ALL ABOUT
LANDSCAPING

Written by
Lin Cotton, ASLA

Edited by
A. Cort Sinnes

Art Direction and Design by
Craig Bergquist

Plan Drawings by
William and Nancy Wilson

Illustrations by
Craig Bergquist
Deborah Russell

Ortho Books

Publisher
Robert L. Iacopi

Editorial Director
Min S. Yee

Managing Editor
Anne Coolman

Horticultural Editor
Michael D. Smith

Production Editor
Barbara J. Ferguson

Editorial Assistant
Maureen V. Meehan

Administrative Assistant
Judith Pillon

Consultants
Jack Chandler, ASLA
   St. Helena, CA
Sid Lewin, ASLA
   San Francisco, CA
James McNair
   San Francisco, CA

Copy Editing by
Editcetera
Berkeley, CA
Typography by
Terry Robinson & Co.
San Francisco, CA

Graphic Production by
CABA Design Office
San Francisco, CA

Color Separations by
Color Tech Corp.,
Redwood City, CA
Address all inquiries to:
Ortho Books
Chevron Chemical Company
Consumer Products Division
575 Market Street
San Francisco, CA 94105

Printed in August, 1980

1 2 3 4 5 6 7 8 9 10

ISBN 0-917102-87-8

Library of Congress Catalog Card
Number 80-66347

Acknowledgements

Harold Biswell, SAF
   Professor Emeritus
   U.C. Berkeley
Jack Buktenica
E. Douglas Chism
Aylett and M. J. Cotton
David Davenport, PhD.
   U.C. Davis
David D. Davis
   Rain Bird Sprinkler Mfg. Corp.
Charles Deaton
Jesse Lelianthal
Stephen Marcus
Kathy Mathewson
Phoebe Cutler Martensen
Oehme, van Sweden &
   Associates, Inc.
   Washington, D.C.
Theodore Osmundson—Fellow,
   ASLA
Robert D. Steiner, AIA
Robert Tetlow, ASLA
Treetops Nursery
   Albuquerque, NM
Robert Turner
Marguerite Viles
   Santa Fe, NM
William Wilson
Betty Wood

Photography by
(Names of photographers are
followed by the page numbers
on which their work appears)
Bill Aplin: 45
Martha Baker: 49
Dennis Bettencourt: 41, 46
John Blaustein: 33
Tom Bradley: 12
Clyde Childress: 11
Josephine Coatsworth: 9, 10, 21,
   22, 34, 48, 58, 59, 70, 73, 74,
   75, 77, 79, 80, 84, 90, 91, 92
Cornell Department of Horticulture:
   22
Mike Landis: 5, 8, 18, 24, 26, 30,
   31, 35, 37, 41, 44, 45, 47, 49, 50
   51, 55, 71, 78, 81, 93, 94, 95
MLTW/Turnbull Associates: 14
Elvin McDonald: 39, 46
Mike McKinley: 6, 7, 14, 17, 19,
   25, 26, 28, 29, 32, 33, 34, 35,
   36, 38, 39, 40, 43, 47, 53, 54,
   57, 67, 78, 79
James McNair: 9, 15, 27, 35, 39,
   40, 53, 57
Picnic Productions: 56
William Reasons: 50
Dick Rowan: 8
Tom Tracy: 4, 10, 23, 33, 36, 37,
   41, 47, 49, 51, 52, 57

Photo Research by
Carousel
New York, NY
Laurie Winfrey
Charlie Holland

Colour Library International (USA),
   Limited: 16
The Image Bank/Harold Lloyd:
   19
Magnum Photos, Inc./Rene Burri:
   21
Photo Researchers, Inc./M. E.
   Warren: 23
Woodfin Camp & Associates/
   Adam Woolfitt: 20

Front and Back Covers
The view of a landscape from directly above is unfamiliar, and yet
landscape plans are made from this
perspective. The two-dimensional
plan of a western landscape on the
back cover comes to life in the
front cover photograph of the
same site.
Photograph by Mike Landis
Plan Drawing by Peter Szasz

ALL ABOUT
LANDSCAPING

KEYS TO A GOOD LANDSCAPE

A successful landscape results from the sensitive balancing of many elements, some of which may surprise you. But the essential first step is for you to decide exactly what you want and what you like, so your landscape design suits your tastes and needs.

This all green garden is more than just a landscape. It serves as a secluded retreat—a hideaway from the hurly-burly activities of the workaday world. Its effect is purposely serene and inviting. Imagine walking barefoot across this lush glade...

The best landscapes reflect the needs and tastes of the owners. If a shady outdoor eating area, combined with a place for the children to play, is what is most important to you, make sure you plan carefully to achieve those spaces.

All homeowners deserve a landscape that brings them pleasure and joy. However large or small your yard or property, you can extend the lifestyle you enjoy inside your home to the environment outside your door. Thoughtful planning can yield a practical and pleasurable living space that only the outdoors can offer, whether you want to sunbathe, swim, play croquet or tennis, barbeque, work, dine in the shade, or just relax in a hammock.

You won't want to overlook the fact that a good landscape also increases the value of your property. But the most important function of a landscape is what it does for you and the other people who live there. Your landscaped yard or garden should be a wonderful place to go to, a place where you can discard your worries and enter that other world of plants. It is in your landscape that you can putter, rest, eat, play... or just sit quietly contemplating the pleasures of the scene around you.

While the advantages of having a beautiful landscape may seem obvious, consider the advantages of also creating this landscape yourself. Landscaping has always carried with it a certain mystique —an art form that seems beyond the reach of the uninitiated. If you have ever thought about landscaping your yard, probably your first reaction was that you would need to call in the professionals and spend a great deal of money.

The premise of this book is that landscaping is not mysterious. You can learn to design a new landscape or improve an existing one, and you can do it for far less money than you would spend if you asked a professional to do it.

What is landscaping all about?

Once you have decided you can do it yourself, you need to define just what landscaping encompasses. A *landscape*, per se, is simply a natural environment that can be designed by nature as well as by people. The art of *landscaping* is the act of purposefully changing the natural features that exist out of doors, with the intention of making the environment more attractive. Those features that are added usually involve plantings, but may also include rock and wood and other natural or human-made materials.

Landscaping can be considered a living sculpture, a work of art that is ever changing with the seasons and growing with the years. Discard any notions you may have about the right, or perfect, or ultimate landscape. The landscape you create should be distinctly your own, and there are as many possibilities as there are people and land.

One of the traditions of western civilization is the notion that one's home is one's castle, which is also an expression of one's self. We want our homes and landscapes to have the colors, fragrances, furnishings, and spaces that we feel comfortable in.

In eighteenth-century England, landscaping was thought to be a form of art equal to painting, literature, music, and drama. Like these other arts, it was considered a unique mode of artistic expression. In formulating your own landscape, you have the opportunity to express your own aesthetic ideas and to put together an environment that pleases and suits you.

Natural beauty

As with other artistic endeavors, when you begin to plan a landscape, your involvement may even begin to transcend your immediate goals: You also have the inestimable pleasure of creating natural beauty for its own sake, and in the process becoming attuned to nature's continuing life cycle. In the Greek myth of the Minotaur, Theseus leaves for Crete to do battle, perhaps to kill the monster Minotaur. His father, the king of Athens, afraid that his son will not return, goes out and plants trees. This king is an old man; so people ask him why he has bothered to plant these trees, since, surely, he will not live long enough to see them grow to maturity. "Ah," he says, "I am planting them for my son. For if Theseus is killed by the Minotaur and never returns, the trees that I have planted will grow and bear fruit and continue in this life." Recognizing the continuum of life in the things we plant, in the landscapes we devise, and in the trees that outlive many human generations, ties us to life forces that are far greater and larger

than our own lives. There is a therapeutic balm in planting things and in establishing places of beauty that will live on in the future, often beyond our lifetimes.

The successful landscape

The first hurdle in any project is getting started, and a big step toward jumping that hurdle is having confidence in yourself. One purpose of this book is to give you all the information you will need so that you will develop confidence in your ability to create a successful landscape.

The key to a good landscape is design, as distinguished from mere decoration. To decorate is to put things into your environment without knowing why you are doing so. There is no real intent, no plan, no essential connection to you, the creator. In comparison, when you *design* a landscape, you *know* why you are putting this plant here and that walkway there. A landscape design is one that you have thought through; your choices are conscious and intentional. Your landscape is an entire stage show, directed to please one audience: you.

A successful landscape is one that does what you want it to. So the place to

start is with you. What do you like? What effects please you and make you feel good?

Think of some place you have been that you have really loved. Perhaps it was your grandmother's garden, or some special place in a park, or sitting on a friend's deck or patio. Wherever it was, that something special, that quality that you liked, made you want to be there. The nature of those special places—the qualities they contained and the feelings you had when you were there—are all elements of landscaping. And you will make a successful landscape to the extent that you can recreate these elements.

The problem is, most of us have no idea of how to create these effects. One of the most helpful things you can do is to begin a scrapbook or a file of ideas that appeal to you. Fill it with notes made from memory, photographs from books and magazines, photographs you take of a garden you pass on a street, clippings from newspapers—it doesn't matter. The point is to assess all the landscaping ideas that come your way in terms of what is pleasing to you. The clearer you are about what you like, the easier it will be for you to create those qualities in your own landscape.

Ideas for landscapes can come from anywhere. This rural field, with its grassy plumes backlit by the sun, was the inspiration for the landscape you see on the facing page.

The purpose of the book

By writing this book we hope to assist you in designing and building a landscape that expresses your tastes and interests, deals with your particular environmental assets and problems, and meets your practical needs. The first five chapters of this book contain information on landscape design that goes beyond that of the standard how-to landscape manual. By helping you to understand the qualities that make a landscape "work," you will not be forced to mold your yard into Landscape Plan A, B, or C, which may or may not have anything to do with your favorite ideas.

At any stage along the way, you may decide to get professional assistance. What you prefer to do yourself and what you want to leave to others depends largely on your own interest and budget. If you mainly want to pursue aspects of design and planning, this book will provide you with the insights and information you will need and will help you to select and supervise contractors for planting and construction.

On the other hand, if you want to do the planting and construction yourself and obtain professional help with the design, this book will provide the construction details you will need and give you a good basis for consultations with a landscape architect. One of the landscape architect's tasks is to help you zero in on exactly what effects you want. By doing some of the preliminary thinking yourself, with the aid of this book, you can use your architect to help you expand and refine the ideas you have already come up with, thereby saving you time and money, and probably frustration.

And if you wish to do everything yourself, from start to finish, this book will help you to do just that.

Every bit as attractive in this tamed setting, the grassy plumes add a dramatic accent to the landscape. Don't be afraid to be experimental. If you see something that pleases you in the wild, try to recreate the effect at home.

The plan of the book

The rest of this chapter is devoted to some general, but important concepts intended to expand your view of what is possible when you create a landscape.

Chapter Two describes and illustrates a selection of landscape styles. Style is usually the first thing you notice about a landscape. This overall statement that a landscape makes differs from fundamental design principles, such as enclosure and space. Seeing these specific examples will allow you to distinguish between style and design and to identify the stylistic features of landscapes that you like.

The elements of design are covered in Chapter Three. These are the very specific "forces" of space, enclosure, color, light, texture, and so on. Understanding the elements that are present in every good landscape, no matter what its style, will make it possible for you to analyze the things you admire in the landscapes that attract you. A knowledge of these fundamental design principles will enable you to manipulate them into the landscape effect you desire.

Plants and materials are your artist's palette. Selecting them carefully is an essential step in forming a landscape. Chapter Four identifies the particular features of plants and materials that you should consider when making your choices.

After you have familiarized yourself with basic design considerations, you can begin to set your plan down on paper. By answering 30 very specific questions, the ideas you have been gathering are bound to come together so that you can order your priorities. Then, with the information in Chapter Five, you can commit to paper anything from freehand thumbnail sketches to professional-looking working drawings, depending on the lengths to which you want to go.

Chapter Six is filled with the tricks of the trade: from clearing and grading the site to installing an irrigation system, to planting and maintaining the last annual —name your problem, you'll find the answers here.

If you spend part of a weekend leisurely reading and looking through this book, you can be well on your way to developing a complete landscape plan. But we also encourage you to take your time; avoid making quick decisions just so that the project will get done in a hurry. In the long run, you will be much more satisfied if you take the time you need to envision exactly what you want.

Once you have a general concept in mind, don't expect to arrive at all the detailed decisions at once. Living with an unfinished landscape may be difficult at first, but as you involve yourself in the landscaping process, you may find that it is more exhilarating to develop exactly what you have in mind than it is bothersome to have some bare earth for awhile.

A LANDSCAPE OVERVIEW

Public and private spaces

Land set aside and designed for the public has a different sort of personality than land intended only for private use. Many privately maintained landscapes are, however, publicly visible. Just as in *Hamlet* Polonius says, "The apparel oft proclaims the man," so do the public aspects of your landscape reflect an image of you.

One of the things you need to decide is which aspects of your landscape you think of as "public" and which ones you think of as private. In some countries, the entire residential environment is considered private; even friends are rarely asked to visit there. In our culture, we use our homes to entertain people we know (and sometimes even those we don't know). So you will want to work out the division of public and private spaces that appeals to you. You may want your entire garden to be on display. Or you may want some degree of separation from street onlookers. Most landscapes compromise these two points of view, devoting some space to public and some to private use. But by making this distinction a conscious one, you will increase your ability to have just what you want.

Openly visible parts of your landscape can usually be converted into private or semiprivate spaces. You may need to build a fence, screen the garden from outside view with carefully chosen shrubs, or perhaps plant some trees to block out a neighboring apartment building. If you are mainly concerned with the way your house looks from the street and the impression it makes on people coming to the door, you will arrange things differently than if you plan for private use.

Sometimes private and nonprivate spaces can be dramatic in their contrasts. In New York's Soho District in Manhattan, some of the city's most fashionable residences are lofts sequestered in dilapidated-looking buildings. Part of the charm of these luxurious hideaways is the juxtaposition of the two extremes. MGM made use of a similar effect in its film of *The Wizard of Oz*. When Dorothy enters Munchkinland, the film switches from black and white to color. You may have the kind of location that permits you to make such contrasts in your landscape. After all, the ideas most suitable to your site won't necessarily come from observing other landscapes; they can come from anywhere.

The borrowed landscape

While it is helpful to make the distinction between public and private land, you can also look at your landscape as actually extending beyond your property's limits. In a sense, the entire world is your landscape, because whatever you choose to notice essentially then becomes yours. Your experience can be as limited or expansive as you choose to make it.

This principle can be applied to the street you live on and your neighbors' yards. You can easily make use of the vistas and vegetation that happen to lie outside of your yard. And, no matter how large or small your own plot is, you can expand it into the neighboring terrain. Distant trees or mountains can be opened to view. Perhaps you and your neighbor can work together to plant masses of trees and shrubs that diffuse the property line. The sense of privacy, security, and independence that a fence and individualized lot-by-lot planting gives can be devised by letting adjacent land merge together, creating much more usable and pleasing space for all.

In Japan, the borrowed landscape is a long-practiced notion. Low, mounding

If you want to use the area in front of your house for privacy, you can do so with a gracefulness that is as appealing on the public side as it is within the private side.

High above a busy street, this backyard oasis is virtually unnoticed by passerbys and neighbors. Sometimes it takes considerable effort to create the private space that you want for outdoor living. In this case, the entire deck and pool had to be cantilevered over the hillside, but for this satisfying result, it was well worth it.

In some cases, where privacy is not a concern, you want to invite the whole outdoors into your yard. This attractive pool and lawn area "borrows" the entire surrounding landscape and creates a dramatic scene. The low wall is all that is necessary to create a feeling of enclosure.

Public areas, visible to pedestrians, passing buses, and automobiles can be dramatically improved with such simple landscaping efforts as the planting of appropriate trees.

shrubs conceal the property limits, but do not destroy the ability to enjoy the surroundings at large. Instead of looking like a quarter-acre lot, a piece of land can be made to look much larger by cleverly locating the house, providing view spaces, and camouflaging the property boundaries with plantings. If you intend to make use of a neighboring landscape, perhaps the worst thing you can do is to plant a straight line of trees along the deed line. By doing so, you are making a statement that nothing beyond your garden matters, and that you want to block out any other view, even if you can't do so effectively.

Neighborhood landscaping

What you do within the confines of your yard also makes an impression elsewhere. The trees you plant will be seen from afar as they grow, and flowers and shrubs will be appreciated by passersby. The attention you pay to the streetscape will eventually have an impact on the atmosphere of your own place. Plant the parking strips, if there are any, and see about planting street trees that will correspond with plantings in your garden. The more you take interest in the space surrounding your home, the more you will, in effect, "own" it.

If you live in an apartment, you can borrow the landscape in another way: by becoming responsible for neglected public areas. For example, you might want to plant bulbs along the roadsides where you can appreciate them from the bus, water street trees, or tend an abandoned patch of greenery.

Neighborhood landscaping can include participating in antilittering efforts and in helping to control tree diseases and pests by spraying and pruning your own plants. As you take care of the larger landscape and show your respect for it, your neighbors may become inspired to do the same. The end result may be a greatly improved landscape for you and everyone else to enjoy.

Sometimes it's hard to see the forest for the trees. By taking advantage of all those elements already present in the landscape, you may find that you really don't have to do very much yourself. Some of the most attractive landscapes are those that are left close to their natural state.

These mature oaks give this landscape its particular flavor and character. By fitting the landscape around the trees, the owners achieved an effect that might have taken years to produce in another way.

Taking advantage of what you have

Often, although a landscape may be well intentioned, it simply does not fit into the character of the neighborhood. It fails to utilize the unique qualities of the site, and follows a plan that could have been used just as well in a hundred other locations. A landscape may not be the most pleasing just because it is unique.

Except in absolutely new subdivisions where the sites are graded, some kind of landscaping, albeit meager, already exists. Whatever this older landscape is—a well-developed planting you want to remodel, a wild country spot with native trees, an apartment courtyard—work toward making your changes fit into the whole.

Make the most of what you have to work with. If you live in a condominium, and a 10-by-20 foot patch of ground is your only space in which to landscape, consider the peculiar advantages of your situation. Your garden can be like a jewel box. Although you won't have room for large trees, you can certainly grow small ones in tubs, you can train vines into an overhead canopy, or add the special atmosphere of a mountain stream with the aid of a simple Japanese splash-box. A limited amount of space needn't hamper your ability to design a charming outdoor area that improves the mood of your home.

On the other hand, you may own a big place in the country that needs landscaping. You will want to consider the possibilities of creating areas that have an intimate quality, modifying the tree cover, siting auxiliary buildings and establishing new roads and paths.

Most outdoor environments fall somewhere in between these two examples. If you have a house on a lot, it will almost certainly have some sort of existing landscape that will need to be assessed in order to use it wisely, without wasting landscaping opportunities.

Respecting the genius of the place

Nature will please you more often if you are alert to its needs and directions, and if you work to satisfy them. Designing a landscape is not only the art of making changes fit into the existing architectural and social spheres, but also of assimilating changes into the physical, biological, and horticultural spheres.

Before artificial plantings and other changes were brought about by housing developments, the character of your area had a special flavor. It may have been a dense, hardwood forest with craggy outcroppings, like Manhattan was in the sixteenth century. Or perhaps it was an open, grassy field, sparsely peppered with giant oak trees. The eighteenth-century poet, Alexander Pope, advised us to respect the "genius of the place" in our gardens and landscapes. This respect demonstrates an attentiveness to and feeling for what is natural. But even if your neighborhood doesn't resemble the wild landscape that you know once existed there, the character or genius that has taken its place must also be respected.

To discover more about the native character of your land, drive out to uninhabited areas close by. Is it flat, rolling, or steep? Is it forested or open? The quality of this native land can serve you in two

Not all of what is significant and beautiful in a landscape is immediately obvious. The ephemeral beauty of fallen leaves wet from the first autumn rain, or the fleeting intensity of a daylily bloom elicit another kind of sensitivity and appreciation. These temporary images lend a very special character to every landscape.

ways. First, it is a sure indication of what grows well in your area. By following these botanical clues, you can plant your landscape with natural forms in mind, which, by the way, reduces landscape maintenance. You actually work against nature when you try plants that don't grow well in your region.

Second, by following the natural landscape trends of your area, your individual landscape will fit in. It will have the right feel and will not stick out like a sore thumb. Your landscape will be a personalized extension of all that nature offers in your locality.

If you want to, you can design a truly native landscape, only using plants that are indigenous to your area. Some gardeners feel that these are the most beautiful landscapes of all. Midwestern landscape architect Jens Jensen says, "To me no plant is more refined than that which belongs. There is no comparison between native plants and those imported from foreign shores which are and should always remain novelties .... Every plant has its features and must be placed in its proper surroundings so as to bring out its full beauty. Therein lies the art of landscaping."

This sentiment may be a bit austere, particularly since native plants can be hard to get and may not suit your particular landscaping tastes. But the concept of using native plants becomes more feasible if it is expanded to include those plants that resemble aspects of the native variations. For example, suppose you live in an area that has a Mediterranean-like climate, in which the native plants are accustomed to a five- to seven-month drought each year. If you put in tropical plants that require considerable summer irrigation, you are inviting extra expense and trouble. If you do so knowingly, you won't be disappointed, but if you are unaware that tropical plants are not well suited to your garden, you may be in for unexpected and unwanted problems. But if you choose plants that you can buy at your nursery or garden center that are similar to those you find in the wild, your landscape is off to a head start.

The ephemeral qualities of nature

Once you begin to expand your sensibilities to your entire environment, you will start noticing things you've never seen before. And once you start noticing them, your interest is likely to be aroused. An appreciation of some of the subtler, more transitory qualities of nature will increase your landscaping possibilities immeasurably.

There's the daylily flower that lasts for only a moment in the life of the garden, the tobacco flower that wafts its sweet scent only at night, the unexpected cluster of mushrooms, the flock of visiting birds feeding on the cotoneaster, the new fall of golden oak leaves and acorns. These are short-lived but special moments in the garden, all of which contribute to the show. Without these ephemeral qualities, the landscape would be much less exciting.

In Japan, the appreciation for subtlety in nature has reached a peak. Before guests arrive, a Japanese may rake and clean the garden, then sprinkle freshly fallen leaves on the raked paths to recreate a natural look.

By specifically planning for some of these delightful but short-lived garden features, you can build in surprises that will make your landscape a more captivating place to be.

A CLOSER LOOK AT LANDSCAPE STYLES

Of the many styles to choose from, we've selected eleven classics to illustrate here. The particular style of your landscape—its "flavor"—will be its most apparent feature, so take the time to make sure it fits your lifestyle and environment.

Matching the style of your landscape to the style of your house can do a great deal for both. This Oriental garden complements the exterior of the house, and helps to achieve a total effect that might be impossible with any other type of landscaping. Partly because of its complex simplicity, the Oriental style can be difficult to attain gracefully.

This house, with its rustic exterior, has a country feeling, even though it is in an urban setting. To strengthen the qualities of the house, an informal, cottage-type garden was planted. The result is a charming picture that delights neighbors and passersby.

On the following pages we present landscapes that differ in almost every way imaginable. These particular examples were selected because they were fine representations of distinct styles, and also because each landscape, in its entirety, contained a certain excellence and appeal that could only be called forceful.

We will describe that forceful quality in more detail in Chapter Three, but generally speaking, it is a quality that resists easy definition. For most people, the force is simply felt by an intuitive reaction to scenes that appear "right and good".

You'll find it very helpful to go beyond that initial intuitive reaction and study the landscapes you see with a discerning eye. What specifically makes the scene appealing? Is it the lighting, the style, the health and vigor of the plants, the colors, the harmonious combination of landscape and architecture, or all those things? Whatever it is that appeals to you, the better you are at describing it, the easier it will be to make it a part of your own personal landscape.

On the following pages you may also see styles that would not normally appeal to you, but because of the excellence in the presentation, you are able to see what makes the style attractive to other people. You may find yourself saying "I would never plant that type of garden, but it certainly looks attractive in that setting".

When you look beyond style, what do you see? In almost every case, the creator of the landscape has held a high regard for certain fundamental design principles. The styles may change, but the need for a solid design remains the same. As you look at each landscape, look beyond the style to see what the fundamental design is: it is the common thread that binds all good landscapes together.

As you look at other landscapes for ideas for your own site, remember too that it's a good idea to stay within the reasonable limits of your native landscape and to be careful about combining a number of styles. There's nothing wrong with electicism, but having a bit of formal box hedge next to a Japanese garden on the edge of a Spanish courtyard with rustic, early American benches would be more than a person could assimilate and unattractive, as well. If your house has an English Tudor exterior, think twice about creating a southwestern desert type landscape. For the most pleasing results, match the style of the landscape to that of the house.

THE WILDSCAPE

One of the best examples of a wildscape can be found surrounding the homes at a development called Sea Ranch on the rugged coastline of northern California. Regulations of the development require rustic exteriors on all the homes, and plantings are limited to native species. In addition to this, the siting of the houses and the forms of the plantings are controlled to allow all of the residents to borrow the entire surrounding landscape. The effect of this sensitive landscape is that it seems to grow out of the site like the great boulders and cliffs of the coast itself. There are no jarring notes, nothing to keep the viewer from appreciating the spirit of the surroundings.

Across the country in Connecticut, a major corporation recently landscaped their headquarters in a similar style. Much of the site was untouched by construction, and by careful management for a period of years, major changes were made in the area's appearance and wildlife population. In effect, the landscaping actually restored the primeval quality of the site.

The forest on this site had grown into a state of decadent climax. Hardwood trees that normally would have been thinned by natural causes, such as fire, crowded against one another and blocked any sun that tried to reach the forest floor. Landscaping in this case consisted of clearing the hardwoods from the cedar groves and planting native wildflowers in new openings that simulated openings caused by fires.

Birds and wildlife were attracted back to the woods, and added a source of color and variety. Among the plants encouraged by the wildscaping were Sargent's crabapple, highbush cranberry, alder, dogwood, hawthorne, elderberry, viburnum, blue flag, Dutchman's breeches, and trailing arbutus. Native stands of pink lady's slippers were preserved and the meadows restored by removing non-native planting that had encroached over the years.

We started off the discussion of different landscape styles with wildscapes because it is important to realize that there are situations where less is more. In both of these instances, in California and Connecticut, a forceful quality was created by respecting and enhancing the native landscape. In both cases, no contrived planting could have created an effect as pleasing, or with as much quality, as the use of native plants where they naturally belong. Mosaics of native plants in landscapes that simulate the primeval character in wildland situations are often the best landscape style.

Two extreme examples of wildscaping: The photograph above shows the housing and landscaping done at Sea Ranch, a development in Northern California. Both the structures and the landscape seem to rise right out of the rugged cliffs. To the right, the delightful complexity of a wild garden in New England. Both reflect the native character of each region.

THE FORMAL LANDSCAPE

Juxtaposed to the all-native landscape is the traditional formal landscape that comes to use from the Age of Reason in eighteenth-century France and England. The rigidity of the formal style, with the clipped box hedges of the *parterre* (see photograph) and its strict attention to geometric forms superimposed on the landscape, with little or no regard for the native character of the site, may strike most contemporary gardeners and designers as a bit too severe for today's way of living. Even so, the formal style has its rightful and deserved place in modern landscapes.

The ordered landscape grew out of a medieval need to economize on space within the walls of manor house compounds, castles and monastaries. Planting within those tight geometric paths and beds was as much a matter of efficiency and convenience as it was the prevailing style.

Monks who grew medicinal herbs in the confines of the safe walls, also made efforts to adorn the houses of God with their plantings. The French kings, their ladies and courtiers, took the simple garden of earlier medieval years and made the grand formal garden. There seemed no limit to the grandeur of these outdoor palaces, mirrors of the image and extravagance of the king's court. More than one of the grand royal garden had two identical plantings; a hidden one being a subterfuge, keeping its fruits, berries and sweet scented flowers for the exclusive enjoyment of the king.

Above: A portion of the famous gardens at Versailles in France. The formal, severely clipped box hedges form a *parterre*. Note how the lake and the landscape in the distance seem to be geometrically carved out of the surrounding forest. Right: A formal garden on a much smaller scale offers intimacy without sacrificing any of the rules of formality.

THE COTTAGE GARDEN

The typical cottage garden appeals to many people because of its casual exuberance and seeming lack of constraints. But even the smallest dooryard garden should have some overall design to it, or it will appear to be a jumble, rather than having the homey character that gives it distinction.

Compared to the French and English formal gardens, the New England cottage garden was a humble effort indeed. While one early settler described his garden as "gay with a variety of flowers, including the fair white lily and sweet fragrant rose," the basic style and contents were dictated by necessity. The picket fence covered with vines and climbing vegetables was erected to separate the garden from the adjoining hillside to keep the sheep away. And the tremendous variety of plants found in the planting beds surrounding the Colonial house was because the seventeenth-century housewife had to grow her own medicinal herbs and household aids, such as cleansing agents, dyes, insecticides, air purifiers, lotions, and cosmetics. In Ipswich, Massachusetts, the restored garden at Whipple House presents a collection of the plants most commonly grown in the early American garden.

Even though these cottage gardens were not intentionally decorative, we tend to see them that way by today's aesthetic standards. It is still a favorite landscape style, particularly for people who enjoy collecting plants. The intricate textures and fragrant surprises of a modern cottage garden can provide endless delight and interest. In various seasons the perennial borders of herbs merge with the bulbs and annuals planted in the main part of the beds. These orderly yet abundant beds are enclosed by tidy, modest paths and fences. And today's cottage gardens usually provide sitting areas adjoining the planting beds, the better to enjoy fragrance and view.

Small gardens with a wide variety of plants need a strong overall design. Without a strong structure, the effect of the garden will probably resemble nothing more than a confused jumble. Before planting anything, decide whether you want a geometric garden composed of straight lines and angles, or a softer scene of flowing curves and rounded forms. Make the design as simple and straightforward as you can; create complexity and interest with the plants themselves.

Try to plan your garden so that there is always something of interest to be admired. It might be fragrant flowers, the bare winter form of a deciduous shrub, or an espaliered pyracantha with its flame-red berries. The cottage garden should present a vibrant, ever-changing show. If you keep a record of when particular plants bloom in your garden, you can combine them with other blooming plants for striking color combinations in future seasons.

FOUNDATION PLANTINGS

Foundation plantings serve the practical purpose of hiding the tall foundations of many older homes, particularly those with first-floor basements. As a style, it has been used in many instances where it is not necessary, and has suffered from overuse. In this particular case, it is well used, appropriate, and offers a pleasing array of textures and shades of green.

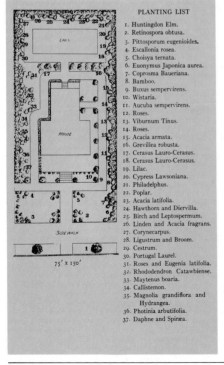

PLANTING LIST

1. Huntingdon Elm.
2. Retinospora obtusa.
3. Pittosporum eugenioides.
4. Escallonia rosea.
5. Choisya ternata.
6. Euonymus Japonica aurea.
7. Coprosma Baueriana.
8. Bamboo.
9. Buxus sempervirens.
10. Wistaria.
11. Aucuba sempervirens.
12. Roses.
13. Viburnum Tinus.
14. Roses.
15. Acacia armata.
16. Grevillea robusta.
17. Cerasus Lauro-Cerasus.
18. Cerasus Lauro-Cerasus.
19. Lilac.
20. Cypress Lawsoniana.
21. Philadelphus.
22. Poplar.
23. Acacia latifolia.
24. Hawthorn and Diervilla.
25. Birch and Leptospermum.
26. Linden and Acacia fragrans.
27. Corynecarpus.
28. Ligustrum and Broom.
29. Cestrum.
30. Portugal Laurel.
31. Roses and Eugenia latifolia.
32. Rhododendron Catawbiense.
33. Maytenus boaria.
34. Callistemon.
35. Magnolia grandiflora and Hydrangea.
36. Photinia arbutifolia.
37. Daphne and Spiræa.

Foundation plantings usually rely on an assortment of shrubs to hide the foundation and basement structures of houses built above ground level. This landscape style grew out of the Victorian period of architecture when first-floor basements were commonplace. It was also used around the bungalow houses that composed much of the residential construction across the United States in the first two decades of this century. And, although inappropriate in most cases, it is now common to see foundation plantings around modern ranch-style houses.

Foundation planting is a particularly appropriate landscape style for restored Victorian and bungalow houses. John McLaren, the longtime director of San Francisco's Golden Gate Park, wrote a popular book in 1908 suggesting certain plantings for the houses of the day, from modest city row houses to great estates. As you can see from the plan at left the McLaren style relied on a regular scheme of planting. In fact, his plans, which were widely followed, even showed exactly how to position shrubs and trees.

Consider how your current landscape uses foundation planting, and whether or not that style really fits your house. If you live in an older bungalow or Victorian house, it's quite possible that your garden was inspired by McLaren's book, and you may wish to consider refurbishing your house's surroundings by accentuating this style. Especially if you already have the basic style to work with, a restored foundation planting can be very charming and elegant.

THE ART NOUVEAU LANDSCAPE

Art Nouveau structures and landscapes emphasized native construction materials and a horizontal repetition of lines. In this Greene & Greene house in Pasadena, California, the Art Nouveau style reached a peak. Note the rock wall and the way the vines seem to tie it to the landscape.

When you walk up the path shown in the above photograph you pass through an opening into another world. The fish pond pictured below sets a tranquil mood, fostering the unhurried contemplation of a peaceful scene.

In the early twentieth century, while Mc-Laren was influencing the style of the American landscape, Charles and Henry Greene, craftsmen architects, were developing a style of landscaping that was, and continues to be, distinctive in its charm. The Art Nouveau school of thought maintained that if a landscape could be instantly understood, or seen completely from one position, it was static and uninteresting. Reflecting this spirit, the Greene brothers constructed buildings that are undulating structures of verandas and patios reaching out in many horizontal directions, like the branches on a tree.

The garden entrances to Greene brothers' houses are indirect and unimposing, often making use of pergolas and arbors. There is a gradual, relaxed sense of arrival as one discovers deliberately spaced places to stop and admire—view spots, nooks and benches, highlighted natural features.

The landscape components are asymmetrical, requiring the viewer's active mental participation to complete the forms, much like the Japanese "Way," in which everything living is necessarily incomplete. Because the design elements cannot be understood in a brief glimpse like the formal parterre or the straightforward planting, the garden around a Greene and Greene house is rich and exciting.

The Art Nouveau style of landscaping respects the inherent qualities of a place, while it combines natural materials such as boulders with humanmade materials such as brick. Planting is designed to blend into the existing natural topography, trees, and water courses, as well as to complement the formalism of the geometric architecture.

Suburban residential landscapes offer many opportunities to employ some of the ideas exhibited in the Greene brothers' architecture and gardens. One of the most important qualities in an Art Nouveau landscape is a sense of separation between chaotic and crowded public areas and the intimate, unhurried feeling that can be achieved in one's own setting. No matter how modest your entry walk or driveway is, you can create this important division by diverting paved surfaces so that they bend around shrub masses or important trees, thus calling attention to the views into and out of the garden.

A contemporary and practical principle of landscaping holds that entry walks should clearly lead to the front door, so that newcomers won't be in doubt about where they are headed. In contrast, an Art Nouveau landscape reinforces private space by not leading visitors directly to an obvious destination. A certain amount of confusion is desirable, since it adds a feeling of mystery and privacy to the landscape.

The technique of design known as *sequence* (see page 32) helps to achieve this Art Nouveau principle. You may want the front door to be visible from the street for security reasons, but well-placed trees and shrubs can ensure at least a bit of mystery in getting to that destination. The entryway will reflect the feeling of Art Nouveau if it is enclosed or appears to be enclosed, protecting the private interior from the public's view.

LANDSCAPES IN THE JAPANESE STYLE

This carefully tended Japanese garden looks almost like a painting when viewed from the inside of the house. Rich in varied textures and forms, the landscape represents the miniaturization of a larger natural landscape. Even from inside the house, its intrinsic interest invites the participation of the viewer.

Like Art Nouveau landscapes, traditional Japanese landscapes and small gardens have a sense of privacy and enclosure. Unfortunately, this style has been largely misinterpreted in American residential plantings.

The stylistic points most representative of a Japanese garden are the miniaturization of the larger natural landscape, the borrowing of surrounding views and foliage to expand the private space (see page 8), and the prominence given to individual features, such as rocks, miniature trees, bridges, and garden structures.

Japanese gardens vary considerably, from the moss garden that features hundreds of different types of mosses under a broken canopy of Japanese maples, to the famous Zen Royan-Ji Temple that has only a few carefully placed rocks within a raked field of coarse, gravelly sand, which is surrounded by a richly aged, tiled wall.

Gardens in the Japanese style carefully employ texture and color, juxtapose geometric and free forms, and contrast enclosure with expansion. (See Chapter Three for discussion of these design elements.) The overall character of such a garden speaks of simplicity and order, but does not sacrifice the intricacies of a natural landscape. This is not an easy style to use well; when handled carelessly, it can resemble a miniature golf course rather than a sensitive reflection of nature.

The famous garden at the Zen Royan-Ji Temple in Japan is powerful in its simplicity. With a few deft strokes and simple forms, it evokes a strong sense of the larger natural landscape. This landscape is a classic example of less being more.

To create a garden in keeping with Japanese concepts, it is a good idea to make a concerted study of the subject. There are a number of excellent books devoted entirely to Japanese landscaping and several wonderful public Japanese gardens in various parts of the country.

THE COURTYARD STYLE

The courtyard is an old architectural form from which distinctive landscape styles have been developed. This enclosed garden, surrounded completely by rooms of the house or partially by high walls shutting out the street, has its origins in ancient Persia. The plans of many Persian gardens are preserved in the classic rug designs.

The act of physically shutting out the hostile surrounding environment and creating a pleasing microclimate is similar to the stress for privacy in Japanese and Art Nouveau gardens. Other important qualities, however, distinguish the courtyard from other landscape styles.

In a courtyard garden, there is almost always a formal use of water. A classic Moorish setting would have shallow axial channels of water flowing from level to level, trickling from carvings patterned after fish scales, and lending the cooling sound of water to the air.

In the courtyard style, fountains are often placed in the center of the enclosed space—dripping, squirting, gushing, or flowing, depending on the availability of water.

Planting in these gardens is usually kept to a minimum. There may be a few shade trees, vines on the walls, and flowering shrubs in beds against the walls and in freestanding geometric patterns. The mood sought for is simplicity and tranquility.

The courtyard style might be a ready solution to obtaining privacy and a peaceful atmosphere if your most desirable sun and space are on the street side of your house. Consider how you might wall in a portion of the space, completing the enclosure with the existing house walls.

The sound, scent, and sight of water was practically essential in ancient Persian gardens. Landscapes made by man were concentrated in walled areas, and the lyrical quality of water helped to relieve the extreme geometry of the gardens. In areas with warm climates, the presence of splashing water can make the garden a much more pleasant place to be.

The gardens in the Alhambra in Spain are classic examples of the courtyard style. No matter what the climate or terrain is like outside the walls, the garden inside is an idyllic place.

VARIATIONS ON THE WALLED GARDEN

The extremely bold architectual statements made by Mexico's Luis Barragan spill over into the landscape. Walls and the presence of water are the common threads linking this with the courtyard gardens of the past, but as you can see, the rest is pure imagination and abstraction.

The courtyard theme has been elaborated on by the Mexican architect, Luis Barragan, in his exciting landscape designs. Barragan believes that gardens should be designed to be used in the same manner as houses—encompassing beauty and taste, an inclination toward the fine arts, and spiritual values. He feels that house and landscape should elicit emotion, rather than express the coldness of an environment designed strictly for convenience.

In Barragan's landscapes, walls take on supreme importance—an importance that goes far beyond their utilitarian function. Walls start, stop, start again, appearing to move randomly into the landscape. With walls, Barragan intensifies the experience of spaciousness and enclosure. For example, while an opening between walls allows a view of the surrounding expanse, the walls themselves provide visual interest and enclosure.

Barragan paints his walls in solid pastels, which contrast with the vivid colors of nature and which reflect the hidden colors of the bright Mexican sun. His landscapes are an interplay of mass and void, shadow and light.

An existential quality pervades Barragan's landscapes. It is as if he gives form to that which is an illusion. In certain light, the walls seem to become the courtyard of long ago, reverberating with memories: a child playing on the hard-packed earth, an old woman pedaling a sewing machine, a smoke-darkened kitchen, all unseen but felt. This ability to capture the spirit of life makes his landscapes particularly magical.

The plain white stucco walls of the traditional walled garden are a perfect backdrop for the vibrant colors of summer annuals. Glimpses of these special gardens, seen through gates and archways, entice the viewer to come closer and explore the special places within.

THE OASIS LANDSCAPE

Frederick Law Olmstead, creator of New York's Central Park, is generally considered to be the father of landscape architecture in America. Olmstead respected the "genius" of the place (see page 10), and considered good landscaping essential to pleasant living environments. He attempted to understand the natural character of a site before setting out to design any improvements. However, once he had a grasp of native conditions, he did not hesitate to impose a strong design on the land. Above all, he sought to create pastoral landscapes, made for people to play in and use well.

One of the styles Olmstead developed and refined is usually referred to as the oasis landscape. Philosophically, an oasis is not that different from the cottage garden, in that it promotes the idea of a bit of lush verdure among the expanse of an otherwise untamed environment. Historically, the notion of the oasis was derived from Moorish and Middle Eastern gardens where water was at a premium.

The oasis theme is well illustrated in Olmstead's plantings in the Quad at Stanford University. There, gardens composed of plants that thrive together easily, with little care or maintenance, are isolated from each other by expanses of pavement. At Stanford, oasis landscaping is also ideally suited to the annual summer droughts so typical of the Mediterranean type of climate in California. This type of planting is popular in arid areas of the country, but will work anywhere that a delightful, low-maintenance garden is desired.

Roberto Burle-Marx's abstract landscapes make use of a wide variety of exotic plant material combined with swirling forms and undulating curves. Formerly a painter, Burle-Marx's landscapes are like giant paintings produced on the ground.

This lush bit of landscape, complete with swimming pool, is a modern-day version of the classic oasis. This particular landscape is in New Mexico, where the native climate is severe. Limiting the cultivated landscape to a small area makes good sense from the standpoint of both maintenance and water conservation, and is a traditional design concept in arid climates.

ABSTRACT LANDSCAPES

Roberto Burle-Marx is a Brazilian landscape architect who creates abstract designs in brilliant colors. Before he started making landscapes, he was a fine arts painter. Burle-Marx simply took that talent and applied it to a much larger canvas.

Burle-Marx is also a horticulturist. He explores the depths of the Amazon and brings out native plants that, in some instances, have never before been identified. He raises his own plants and carries out each design in an exciting display of tropical flora. His style emanates from considering the flower as a decorative unit. Gradually, as he composes his landscape bouquets, he discovers and assimilates an infinite variety of color combinations and relationships.

Burle-Marx's landscapes have an abstract, surrealistic feeling that he integrates well with the forms he uses—water, stone, ceramics, and paving materials. They are symbolic landscapes: the perceptible giving form to the imperceptible.

Burle-Marx sees the abstract landscape as an alternative to the symmetrical landscape. Forms like the circle, which Plato called the most perfect of all forms, hold a predictability that Burle-Marx works to avoid. The abstract landscape is bold and aggressive, full of sinuous curves, making mosaics that resemble the wild, curling forms of a meandering river or the natural pattern of lichen colonies. Patterns are composed of texture and color which contrast to the swirling forms of pavement and water courses.

The abstract landscape is a distinct style that requires its own territory, like a blank canvas. If crowded by other landscape styles, the abstract will appear to

Frank Lloyd Wright's famous Fallingwater in Pennsylvania is a good example of imposing an extremely abstract form on the native landscape. The contrast is so strong, that both elements—the structure and the surrounding landscape—are intensified.

PERSONAL LANDSCAPES

A landscape created for a specific individual or family usually has a character that reflects personal tastes and needs. The noted American landscape architect, Thomas Church, made his greatest impact on the American landscape when he opened up the house to the landscape, and vice versa. He created superb landscapes that responded directly to the needs of his clients.

Church's strong designs juxtapose geometric forms with free forms and deliberately enhance a landscape's personal feeling. After many years of creating successful landscapes, Church gathered together some of his best designs into a book entitled *Your Private World: A Study of Intimate Gardens* (San Francisco: Chronicle Books, 1969). In it he encourages readers to develop a landscape that will fit their lifestyles and the sites they are working with.

As you continue your exploration of the various landscape styles, consider how they reflect and serve their users. And, in the process, don't forget to think about how these styles may pattern to your own location and needs.

be a silly imposition of unrelated forms. But given space of its own—perhaps to emphasize features of an untouched landscape nearby, or to contrast with a rigidly geometric architectural form—the abstract landscape can be full of natural force.

Most suburban lots are probably too small to do justice to an abstract landscape and there can be compatibility problems with neighboring landscapes. Nonetheless, Burle-Marx's heightened respect for and awareness of plant forms and colors are a good lesson in seeing plant materials with fresh eyes. Many innovations and combinations are possible when you approach plant form and color with the eyes of a child—full of awe and delight.

Another designer who made the connection between abstract forms and nature was Frank Lloyd Wright. At Fallingwater, one of his designs in southwestern Pennsylvania, Wright attempted to bring people and nature together in an easy relationship. To accomplish this, he invited the landscape into the house—or perhaps it was the other way around.

In 1935 he started to plan and build this architectural creation that would eventually span a waterfall and cling to rocky ledges affording unchecked views into the adjacent woods. The structures seem to grow out of the site.

Wright understood the value of enclosure; even though the Fallingwater house is surrounded by broad bands of windows, the interior is as sheltered as a deep cave. Abstract planting beds are dissected by window walls, helping to tie the surrounding forest to the house's interior.

Making outdoor spaces into living spaces is a comparatively recent phenomenon in landscape design. There was a time when all outdoor spaces were gardens—nothing more and nothing less. Now, the outdoors is invited in, and the indoors invited out.

THE ELEMENTS OF DESIGN

No matter what style you like, a successful landscape requires the use of basic design principles. If you know what the elements are and how to use them well, you can create just the feeling you want.

When viewed from above, the design of a landscape becomes very apparent. Paths, lawns areas, connections from one area to another, mass plantings of shrubs and the shadow pattern of trees all come into sharp focus. When designing a landscape, it will help if you imagine what it will look like from this vantage point.

This carefully designed landscape uses many of the elements discussed in this chapter. Note the pleasant effect of the gently sloped lawn; the graceful repetition of curves; the use of fine-textured plants in the foreground and coarser-textured ones in the background. Although you would never guess it, the curved paths toward the rear of the lawn only continue for a few more feet before stopping at the property line.

Designing a landscape that works

Take a moment to conjure up the image of a favorite landscape—either a real one you remember vividly, or an imagined one. If you look at this landscape in detail, with an eye for identifying the various components that make it complete, what do you see?

You will notice the plants: the trees, shrubs, vines, annuals, and whatever else is growing there. Another obvious element will be the physical confines of the lot: the fences and hedges that define the property line. And, surely you'll see the house and whatever outdoor living areas that already exist, such as patios, walkways, decks, overhead structures, and the like.

Now, pretend you are viewing this landscape from a hot air balloon that's a few hundred feet off the ground. You can see how your neighbor's trees cast large shadows across the lawn, and how the tall hedge blocks a marvelous view of that far-off stand of towering pines. When viewed from this height, is an overall design apparent? Are the outdoor living areas clearly defined? Does the texture, color, size, and form of the plants create an interesting, balanced whole? Is the garden designed for people, with places for the activities that really make a garden alive? And, lastly, is there a single style that predominates? If so, does it complement the house, and as you look out to the larger landscape, does the style of this one, small microcosm fit in comfortably with the surrounding whole? The purpose of imagining a landscape from above is to provide an all-inclusive perspective which takes all the elements of a landscape into consideration. It is the degree to which each of them is successfully treated that makes one landscape more appealing than another.

However, creating a landscape is not simply an ordered process of working with a known set of elements. As with any other creative project, the whole of an especially pleasing landscape more than equals the sum of its parts. In a successful landscape, the individual elements form a chorus, and the finished scene fairly vibrates with vitality and beauty. Truly memorable landscapes—both natural and humanmade—are ones that make an impression on the viewer on many different levels, some of which are quite subtle. For the sake of simplicity, we refer to this subtle quality as the "force" of a landscape.

These memorable landscapes occur frequently in nature, but it is entirely possible for this subtlety to be present in designed landscapes as well. To create this force, the designer must be sensitive to how all the elements that compose a landscape combine. Take another look at the photographs in Chapter Two. In addition to showing distinct landscape styles, each example also contains that force that pulls everything together into a unified, integral whole. If there is magic in design, this is it: the ability to perceive and recreate a balance of the forces that abound so freely in nature.

When this force is missing, the result is often called *visual ambiguity*—the product of uncertain intentions. When a landscape is without intent, the materials and space do not seem to hang together in balance, and the landscape is, therefore, not pleasing.

The design process

Designing and creating your landscape can be as much a source of pleasure as the final product. This process of designing is actually the development of thought about a physical situation that you want to change. The design process begins by opening your mind to new ways of understanding the landscape that you already have. The more conscious and familiar you become with your site and the possibilities for modifying it, the more opportunities it will present to you.

Before you think about what you want your landscape to look like, be sure you know what's there to begin with and how you feel about it. The three steps that lead to these conclusions are called: survey, evaluation, and synthesis. A *survey* is a collection of all the information that relates to a problem. Surveying involves assessing the basic conditions of a site—the topography, existing plants, buildings, walks, and other permanent conditions; discovering what plant materials are available; and determining the desires of the people who will use the site.

To *evaluate* is to order your priorities, deciding what is most important and what can be postponed for awhile. Evaluating is something the avid gardener or true landscaper never really finishes. As you have new ideas, or as your needs and tastes change, the landscape will also undergo change. Reevaluating your landscape is a constant, but pleasant task.

Synthesis is the result of sifting the information gathered during surveying and evaluation. With a firm grasp on what your landscape holds and what priorities you have, you can begin to design! We recommend that you familiarize yourself with the design elements that follow, then examine your present landscape, element by element. This process will give you ideas for viewing your landscape that you never had before and will offer a solid basis on which to make design decisions.

THE ELEMENTS OF PERSPECTIVE

View positions

View positions are the particular spots from which you regularly view your landscape. For intance, one view position might be from your kitchen table, where you sit each morning and evening and look out the window at your garden. Another might be the patio looking West and South, or the front walk leading to the door. Most landscapes have many view positions. To make them easier to identify, the vantage points of these positions have been grouped into three categories.

The view from above has a number of unique qualities. Remember, as a child, how you spied out of a second-story dormer window onto the garden below, and how it made you feel in command of the situation, able to see things that the people on the ground were blind to? The view from a treehouse or a hillside deck can have a similar exhilaration. And, if you've ever had to get up on your roof, you've probably noticed how different your garden looks from there. When you look down, you get a feeling of space, which is sometimes accompanied by a lack of physical security—a feeling that you might fall.

The level view is the position from which we view the world most often. When we experience things on the horizontal plane, the scale of the objects in the landscape and the shadows they cast are the most familiar to us. The level view is moderate and safe; less exciting than others, perhaps, but the one that's the most efficient and the most used in landscapes.

The view from below is the position you find yourself in when your yard is surrounded by high buildings, your house is situated in a canyon, or your patio is built right next to a hill. Viewing the landscape from below may provide a feeling of security or enclosure; or it may feel oppressive. Being aware of the potentials and drawbacks of this position will help you to decide whether there is a place for it in your landscape.

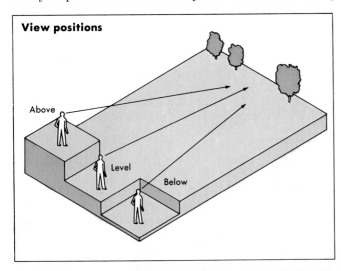

View positions

Above

Level

Below

Opposite page, top: The view from above can make you feel insecure or give you a feeling of power. The viewing platform toward the rear of the yard gives the owners an opportunity to see the surrounding landscape from this unique position.

Opposite page, below: The view from below can contribute to a feeling of security and enclosure.

Right: The level view is the most common and "safe" view in the landscape.

Ground fields

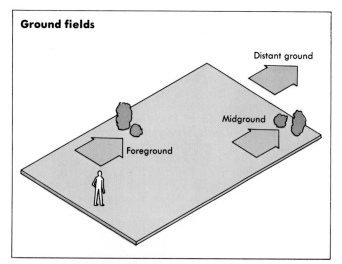

Forcing perspective

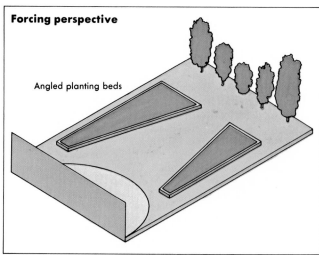

Planning for different textures to be placed in the different ground fields of the landscape is one of the finer points of making a garden pleasant and interesting.

Ground fields

When you stand in one place in your garden, what relationships do the things that you see take on? What you see in the *foreground* is far more detailed than what you can detect in the *distant ground*. The *midground* has more clarity than the distant ground, but not as much as those objects in the foreground. It is important to notice how these perspectives change as you move about in the landscape. Try identifying the ground fields from your favorite view positions, and try to figure out what it is about the perspectives you see that you like.

Forcing perspective

When you force perspective, you can make the midground objects appear to be in the distant ground by reducing their size or by giving them finer textures. By textures we mean leaf patterns or shadow depth, or any other quality an object has that seems to establish its scale relative to the surrounding landscape. In the theater, the further upstage a piece of scenery is placed, and the smaller and more delicately the forms are painted, the greater is the illusion that the scene is far away. And, here's another technique borrowed from the theater: If you have a yard that's deeper than it is wide, and you would like to make it appear even deeper, you can force the perspective by angling the planting beds toward the rear of the garden (see illustration).

The cone of sight

In outdoor rooms, there is a zone of horizontal vision, called the *cone of sight*, that comprises the space from the ground level to about 8 feet above it (see illustration). When you interrupt the view within this zone, such as with a deck railing, a fence, or most other physical enclosures, you bring the feeling of enclosure closer—sometimes too close.

You may have a situation in which you want both a close-in enclosure and a distant view. To do this, you will need to interrupt some of the cone of sight to create the feeling of a nest, but the area above about 2½ feet off the ground should be left open to the view. If you are building a railing for a deck that is more than 3 feet from the ground, the federal Uniform Building Code requires a railing 36 inches high with no opening greater than 9 inches in the railing. (Be aware that this code may vary from state to state, or from county to

This photograph shows in detail the farthest end of the garden shown on page 25. The teahouse and weeping cypress next to it appear to be much farther away from the viewer than they actually are: In reality, the tea house is only six feet tall and the cypress is a dwarf form of a much larger variety. In effect, it creates the illusion of a deeper lot. It is an excellent example of forced perspective.

county.) This rule is intended to keep children from falling from high decks.

To meet the requirements without producing the effects of a cage, make only part of the 36-inch space solid. One formula is to leave about 3 inches at the bottom open to sweep leaves and other debris through, followed by a solid panel 1 to 2 feet wide that runs the entire horizontal perimeter of the deck. Above that, a simple capping of 2-by-6 inch lumber, leaving a 9-inch opening, will complete the height requirement.

The line of sight

In about the middle of the cone of sight there is a zone of particular importance called the *line of sight*. It is the horizontal view either from a standing or sitting position, and is usually between 3 and 6 feet above the floor. Obstructions to the view beyond the line of sight, especially if they occur *only* in this zone, can be very discomforting. This is particularly true if the view is open both from below and above. If you have to block the line of sight for more than a few inches, consider blocking it completely and intentionally with a wall or fence.

The cone of sight

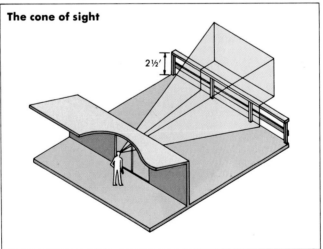

2½'

The axis of the landscape

When you sit on a bench in the garden or a chair on the patio, you tend to look at certain things or in certain directions. What you are doing is focusing on things according to what attracts your line of sight. This visual orientation is called the axis of the landscape.

In formal landscapes, axes and cross-axes form pleasing patterns, partly because of their strong geometric simplicity and partly because they emphasize the naturally straight line of sight. This straightness of vision is the reason garden sculpture or specimen plants should be placed at the end of axis lines, where our eyes will invariably come to rest.

In an informal garden, axis lines are created by suggested lines of sight. While they aren't apparent, they are still important. Suggested axes may be formed by pavement patterns, night lighting, the shape of a clearing through the woods, lawn areas, foliage patterns, and many other contrived and natural occurrences. Even though only suggested, the interconnections of axes can be quite powerful, particularly if they are emphasized and remain uninterrupted. For example, a specimen shrub can be pruned to open up a distant view. And strategic placement of a few containers of plants will help to move the eye along an entryway, and from another direction, provide focus for a flower bed. As you study your site, look for the

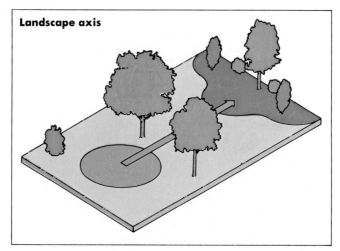

Landscape axis

naturally occurring axes and for ways of strengthening them.

Mystery

Mystery in space is pleasing as long as there is some suggestion of a solution. It is never pleasant to enter a maze when no escape route is evident. Baffled walls lend an air of mystery to any landscape, because they keep you from seeing exactly what lies beyond them. A baffle can be a series of vertical panels, 6 or 8 inches wide and about 6 feet high. As you walk past the louvers, you have just a hint of what is on the other side, flickering past you like an old-time movie.

Another spatial trick is to extend the ground plane out of sight around a solid object. An axis of the landscape may end where a lawn disappears around a mass of shrubs, so that the viewer wonders where the lawn actually ends. The appearance may be that the lawn extends for some distance, when in reality it ends a few feet behind the shrubs.

A lawn that disappears is interesting to look at precisely because we can't see all of it. Paths in the garden and private sections of decks and patios can also take advantage of similar design tricks, disappearing from sight, perhaps to reappear later in another part of the garden.

The mature plantings and placement of the swimming pool in this landscape reinforce its natural axis. Strengthening the line of sight creates a powerful, strong design.

A curved path leading to a known destination creates mystery and heightened interest. Plantings that might otherwise go unnoticed become spotlighted in a subtle way.

Relative size

Outdoor rooms are the most successful when their size is related to their intended use. For example, an intimate private patio should probably be about the size of an intimate sitting room indoors. A barbeque cooking and eating area intended for entertaining should be about the same size as a kitchen-dining room combination that's considered comfortable inside the house.

If your style of entertaining calls for large interior rooms, your outdoor should probably also be large. Or, if you wish your interior rooms were larger, you may want to make the outdoor rooms as large as possible—but be careful. There's a tendency to make outdoor spaces much bigger than they need to be. This can lead to uncomfortably large spaces, with no feeling of enclosure.

The most desirable places to sit outdoors are like the backwaters of a stream, where the water eddies out of the way of the fast-moving water. If you find yourself huddling to the side of your outdoor enclosure, it is probably too large a space in which to feel comfortable.

Try creating smaller spaces within a larger one by placing tubs of plants or groupings of furniture to simulate edges of space. If you find that you like the modification, make it more permanent by alternating the pavement with planting beds and filling them with plants of a pleasing height. If you are redoing your landscape, look critically at the living spaces you have, and be daring: Make them smaller, or larger, or move them to a different part of the yard if you have to.

When planning the size of outdoor rooms, there is a tendency to make them too large. The best advice is to make them approximately the same size as a similar indoor room. This outdoor cooking and eating area has comfortable proportions.

Human scale

General rules about space have so many exceptions that they are useful only as starting points. On one such rule is that space is the most comfortable to people when it has a relationship to the scale of the human form.

An enclosed space takes on human scale when the wall height equals $\frac{1}{2}$ to $\frac{1}{3}$ the width of the space. When walls are less than $\frac{1}{4}$ as high as the width, the area may not appear to be enclosed or to have any scale at all.

A landscape can achieve relative human proportions whether the scale is large or small. A miniature rock garden can be to scale, just as much as a large garden with a view of mountains in the distance. This garden will have human scale if the area is open and wide enough for the distant mountains to have a balancing effect. However, if this yard is narrow and lined on both sides by tall trees, the mountains will appear too tall in proportion to the size of the lot.

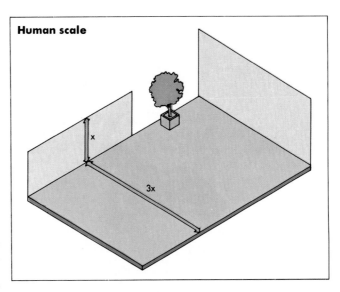

Human scale

Connections

A landscape is influenced not only by open space and enclosure, but also by the way you enter and pass from one area to another. When you plan a landscape, keep in mind that the easy flow of areas, one to the other, is central to their enjoyment.

Consider the close connection between a tool shed and a vegetable garden, the vegetables to the kitchen, the barbeque center to the family room, the hot tub to the lanai or master bedroom. These connections are called *liaisons. Circulation* is how all the liaisons are interconnected —it comprises how you get into, around, and through the landscape: the paths, patios, boardwalks, meanderings across the lawn, stepping stones through a planting bed.

When you begin to outline your landscape on paper, first you may want to conceptualize different ways in which the areas in your yard can relate to each other. This is called *bubble diagram* (see page 64), because you need to think only about the general character of these spaces and their uses. By arranging them in various patterns, you create different liaisons. For example, you may discover that you can open up the dining room by adding French doors, providing access to the patio and outdoor cooking area. By doing bubble diagrams, some connection you had not noticed before may suddenly become obvious.

The circulation can sometimes be thought out in advance, but actual use is the best determinant of where all the connections to liaisons should be placed. It is preferable to get accustomed to where liaisons are, then add paths based on where the ground is the most worn. One junior college was completely pathed in this way; after the first few months of student use, the most popular lines of travel were clearly indicated.

Usually, the shortest route between two places is the best one, if your getting between them is strictly a matter of utility. A landscape designed with aesthetics in mind may eliminate the most evident paths, however, and let them wander by important trees, around garden sculpture, or past revealing views.

Sequence

In the residential landscape, there should be a general indication of which path leads to the front door, but excitement, even mystery, can be developed if the direction is handled in a less than straightforward manner, perhaps heading off at right angles to the door for a bit before returning to its more obvious destination. See pages 18 and 19 for the way this concept is used in certain landscape styles. Landscape architect Lockewood de Forest ordered the sequence of views from the entry drive-

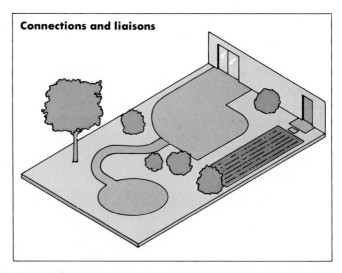

Connections and liaisons

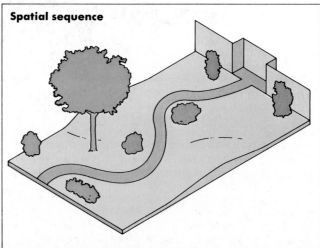

Spatial sequence

Plan walkways to provide a sequence of visual experiences for the enjoyment of those who travel the path. This bench even encourages people to stop and enjoy the scene.

THE ELEMENTS OF FORM

way of a large estate by alternately revealing the house across sweeping lawns, then concealing it behind masses of shrubs, from time to time showing off a specimen tree or rustic bench nestled in the hedgerow.

Changes of scene can make the process of getting to the front door an adventure that's rich in sensory experiences. Each site has its own possibilities; try making a few bubble diagrams to see what kinds of sequences you can come up with for your front yard.

Form relationships

Forms fill the landscape—the plump slope of a hillside, the crown of a mature oak, a marigold blossom, a redwood tree, an A-frame house, a topiary garden sculpture, a cubed outline of a skyscraper, a lean-to shed, a drain inlet, the face of a cliff, a juniper, the repetition of hill upon hill upon hill receding in the distance, the symmetry of a grove of trees—everything has form.

A successful landscape contains forms that balance and complement each other. Too much height, too many curves, too many rectangles, and so on, may not only be ugly, but also make the viewer uncomfortable.

Forms also need to relate well according to their *size*. A circular flower bed that is 10 feet in diameter might work well next to a bed that's 5 feet across, because there is a significant difference in size between

the two. But if you place circles together that are 10 and 8 feet across, your effort will look like you made a mistake, because there isn't enough difference in size to create an interesting contrast.

In the same vein, try to use angles repetitively, but be careful not to mix up angles of too many sizes in a limited amount of space; it will weaken your design considerably. Stay with *angle families*, such as 30-60-90 degrees or 45-90-180-360 degrees. When you plan for odd angles, try to tie them into right angles at some point.

Reinforce two-dimensional forms, such as a circular lawn or a rectangular patio, with three-dimensional masses of shrubs and other solid forms. For example, if you lay out a circular lawn, make the walk around it circular, too, and plant the trees and shrubs in curved patterns that accentuate the main design.

When you are planning a landscape sometimes it is a good idea to stand back and look at the various elements in terms of form only.

What forms please you? Can you introduce them into your landscape, repeating and contrasting them with other forms?

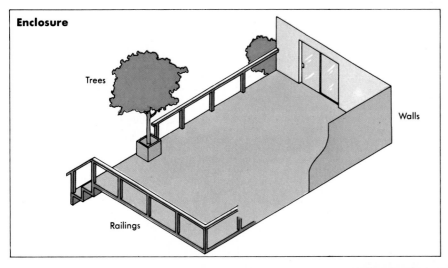

Enclosure

Trees

Walls

Railings

Enclosures

The edges of an enclosure usually produce the feeling of safety and security, the feeling of being in a nest. If a space is too enclosed, however, you'll have the uncomfortable sensation of being in a cage. Natural boundaries, such as canyon walls and banks of foliage from trees and shrubs, can provide the landscape with a sense of security. Similar effects can be created by fences and walls of other structures.

You don't actually have to enclose a space for it to have the feeling of protection and comfort. Enclosure may come from something as simple as an umbrella, tent, or gazebo. Low-mounding shrubs, a rock outcropping, or a depression in the earth caused by the roots of an old tree can feel protective, even though they do not formally enclose anything.

Nor does enclosure have to be from the level position. The partial enclosure from above of the boughs of a tree, or a trellised vine growing overhead provide the sought-after comfort of a kind of nest.

Enclosure does not actually have to provide safety to be effective. On a pier over water, a heavy chain rising from the decking to 2-foot-tall bollards can provide an adequate sense of security, when in reality, they do little to actually ensure it. In the same way, the low guardrail along the outside edge of a treacherous mountain pass makes drivers feel safer.

Providing a sense of enclosure is one of the most important aspects of designing landscape. Without it, the landscape can be uncomfortable and uninviting. Enclosure can be achieved with walls, partial walls, overhead trellises and vines, or simply by emphasizing one corner of a landscape with plants in containers and cascading foliage.

Slopes

A slope is neither horizontal nor vertical, but a slant somewhere in between the two. A landscape is significantly influenced by how the ground slopes. Natural or designed slopes affect the way areas are used and the views available from them. The practical considerations of drainage and grading are covered in Chapter Six.

Tilted surfaces add interest to a landscape. They often provide a sense of enclosure, and tend to intensify the play of light, color, and shadow. On the other hand, if a slope gives the impression that something might fall on you, it usually creates a negative sensation in the viewer.

Even minor changes in incline can be very noticeable. A 3 percent grade (a ⅜-inch drop for every 12 inches of length) doesn't sound like much of a tilt, but it is the maximum allowable on the Interstate Freeway System, even as it crosses the Sierra Nevada, the Rockies, and the Ozarks. Compared to level ground, a 3 percent slope can be as disturbing as a painting that is askew on a wall. When planned carefully, though, a slightly tilted plane can be perfectly appropriate, providing just a hint of enclosure. Hedges and railings are common subjects of this technique. A battered surface is a wall which slopes away at a greater-than-90-degree angle between the ground and the top of the surface. It reflects more light than a simple vertical surface and implies strength. Walls and hedges appear to have more solidarity if they are given this shape.

This landscape gives the feeling of privacy and comfort. These characteristics are reinforced by the slope to the left of the yard. The trees act as an extension of the slope, giving it an even greater effect.

Planning a landscape around a naturally occurring slope requires a little extra thought and effort, but as you can see in these photographs, slopes provide inherent interest and character.

Slopes

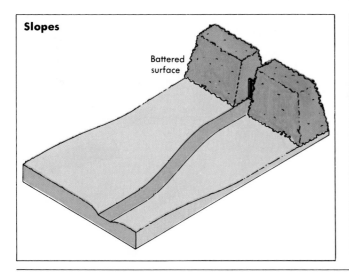

Battered surface

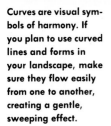

Curves are visual symbols of harmony. If you plan to use curved lines and forms in your landscape, make sure they flow easily from one to another, creating a gentle, sweeping effect.

If you use angles in your landscape design, they should all be in the same family, such as 45-90-180 degrees. Hard-edged geometry can provide contrast to loose forms of natural-style paintings.

The strong use of both vertical and horizontal elements gives this landscape a strong character with clear intentions. There is no doubt that the decked path leads to the house in the background.

Symbolism in form

Forms have deep-seated symbolic connotations that we all intuitively comprehend. Vertical forms induce a state of awe. You may be able to capitalize on this feeling by planting a column of trees, placing a slender statue in the garden where it will show off to advantage, or painting the high wall of your garage to exaggerate its height.

Diminutive and intricate forms tend to evoke curiosity and interest, as in miniature gardens or the patterns in a detailed pavement design.

The static nature of the horizontal line promotes feelings of peacefulness or passivity, and gives the appearance of permanence: Water rests in the horizontal.

Eighteenth-century garden designers believed that the geometric forms made from straight lines were the ultimate expression of Reason, representing the straightforward character of nature. A square lawn, a rectangular pattern made

of box hedges, angled planting beds, a geometrically interesting patio—all have impact on a landscape.

Circular forms have a feeling of closure. Like islands or eddies in a stream, circles are complete in themselves. A circular design in an entryway implies that it is a place to wait, complete in itself. When the door opens, the circle is broken, along with the sense of closure.

Curves are visual symbols of harmony. A garden has many curved shapes in it: leaves and pebbles, a billowing mass of foliage, a rolling terrace. When you design a paved walkway or the edges of a narrow planting bed, give them gentle, sweeping motions that flow from one to the other.

Projecting and jagged forms suggest dynamism and may imply speed and strength. Depending on how they are used, they may also merely look sloppy. Projecting forms can imply power. A cantilevered deck, for instance, whose footings are not

visible, will seem to defy gravity.

Low, shelflike, covered forms, such as caves and canopied walks, imply protection. Contrarily, the freedom of the open desert under starry skies can be oppressive in its abundance, causing us to yearn for mountains or buildings that have the capacity to hold us in. In a very open and level site, the juxtaposition of open to covered spaces makes both independently more interesting.

THE ELEMENTS OF THE SENSES

Microclimate

A microclimate is the fairly uniform climate that is usual for your locality or site. Microclimates can also refer to pockets of modified climate within one site. Climate is made of temperature, relative humidity, and wind. The importance of the microclimate cannot be overemphasized. When you plan where to plant a shrub that requires full sun, where to build your deck, even where to place major walkways, the appropriateness of the microclimate will have a great deal to do with whether your design is successful.

The microclimate of a landscape is influenced in four ways: the presence or absence of direct sunlight, the temperature of the still air, the relative humidity, and the amount of wind. The outdoor comfort range generally lies between 70° and 80°F, as long as the relative humidity is between 20 and 50 percent, and the wind less than 3½ miles per hour.

The higher the humidity rises, the more uncomfortable high temperatures become. Wind can reduce the effects of humid weather; however, where wind velocity goes beyond about 3½ miles per hour, it will probably feel too windy to be comfortable. If you live in a hot, humid climate, look for ways that you can provide areas shaded from the sun, or ways to make the most of cooling drafts.

Strikingly different directions and velocities of wind occur at different elevations. Wind speed close to the ground is usually slower. The wind at 1 foot above the ground may be only ½ that at 6 feet off the ground. When the wind is obstructed, it will slow down even further. Even a 2-foot barrier can cut off most ground wind; keep this in mind if you are planning to build a deck or patio in a windy location.

Wind cools down temperatures and carries sound. So, get to know the wind patterns in your landscape to take advantage of that summer breeze or best avoid that winter turbulence, and to enhance or shield yourself from certain sounds or noises.

Air basins

When cool air moves over land, it moves downward, from higher to lower elevations. Fog is a dramatic example of this process where it can be seen traveling down mountain sides and collecting in valleys and canyons. It's common for cool night air to become trapped in low pockets held in by hills and buildings. If your house is near the bottom of a hill, you may want to build your deck on the uphill side of the house, because the night air will be colder on the downhill side.

Correspondingly, warm air moves upward, from lower to higher elevations. To

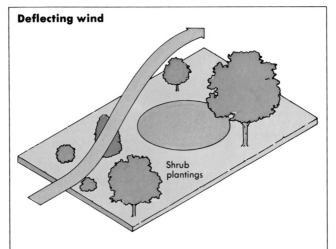

Deflecting wind

Shrub plantings

By locating outdoor living areas such as patios and decks where they will retain the most heat, they can be enjoyed even on cool evenings.

In warm climates, you can take advantage of the fact that cool air collects in basins by siting living areas in the lowest point in the landscape.

help an area retain warmth, you can provide ways for heat from the sun to absorb into surfaces that will release this warmth at night. For instance, the sun's heat is the most intense when it falls on surfaces that are tilted at an angle perpendicular to the sun. Solar panels are angled to take advantage of this fact. A wall angled to collect direct sun will be warmer than an adjacent vertical wall. Absorbed and reflected heat can noticeably warm the surrounding area.

When you choose building materials for any structures, take into account how much heat they retain. For example, stone has low conductivity; wood is a medium conductor of heat; and fiberglass hardly retains heat at all.

Heat absorption is affected by other factors, as well. Materials that are dark or wet tend to absorb more heat than ones that are light in color or dry. Most natural surfaces are relatively heat absorbent.

One of the most striking lighting effects occurs when a canopy of leaves is backlit by the direct rays of the sun. Trees with light-colored foliage are particularly good candidates for this effect.

The shade under mature trees provides welcome relief from the sunny patio surrounding this swimming pool. When designing a landscape, it is important to plan for both sun and shade areas.

The sound of water adds another dimension to the landscape. A simple Japanese splash box may be all that is necessary to mask the unpleasant noise from a neighboring street.

Light and shadow

The quality of light and shadow varies according to the sun's orientation to your site and the ability of the light to reach the ground. In your particular location, the amount of light you receive during the course of a single day will have a tremendous influence on how you design your landscape. If your site is too enclosed by tall trees, you may want to consider ways of allowing more light to filter through. It's hard to realize how important the interplay of light and shadow is on what we see: apparent size and temperature can increase or decrease, and complexities of line and texture can be highlighted or dulled.

Light that strikes surfaces can be described in terms of front, side, and back light. Front lighting emphasizes what is in front and reflects onto and brightens darker surfaces in the background. Side lighting heightens contrast and can produce silhouettes. The most dramatic back-lighting show occurs twice a day when the sun rises and sets against the horizon. Another example of back lighting is when the sun's rays fall through a canopy of leaves. Back lighting is a popular night-lighting technique. Lights hidden behind a solid barrier focus diffused light behind foliage or objects of interest. Pay attention to shadow patterns caused by your house and trees, as well. They can influence your decisions about where to position sitting areas, what construction materials to choose, and what plants to grow.

Sound

Sound is carried by the movement of air. And, like heat, sound can be conducted or not, depending on whether the things around the sound source deflect or absorb it. You can foster the splashing sound of a nearby stream or the rustling of a large tree by making sure nothing blocks the air flow from the stream or tree to where you want the sound to carry. You can muffle street noise by building solid fences or walls that will stop the movement of sound toward you. Sometimes you can mask unpleasant sounds with more musical ones, such as leaves moving in the wind or falling water.

Color

Colors are actually qualities of light. Both the intensity of sunlight and the quality of shadow affect the reflectability of colors in your garden. On an overcast day, colors will appear more muted; on a bright, summer day, colors will be very vivid. These changes in the colors around you may affect your mood, perhaps unconsciously: You may feel depressed on a gray day and vivacious on a sunny one. Colors also change perspective. Light, cool colors enlarge space, while dark, warm colors make areas appear smaller. Blue and gray appear farther away than dark green and red.

Because different colors have profoundly different effects in the landscape, the palette should be chosen with care. There are many colors in this planting, but they were deliberately chosen for their muted tones.

When you think of color in the landscape, don't overlook some of the more unusual combinations: the vibrant fall display of leaves and berries, plants with gray and silver foliage, the classic all-green garden, and a pastel palette of small blossoms.

Fragrance

The sense of smell, like hearing and seeing, is one way to gain access to the wonders of the landscape. If you have to deal with constant sources of unpleasant odors, such as exhaust fumes from a busy street or the odor from a chicken coop, place areas of major human use upwind from them, if at all possible. Ephemeral scents, such as certain vines, shrubs, and trees, will camouflage bad smells as well as add force to the landscape. Plan to place your most fragrant plants where they will do the most good. If you are planning to have a hot tub that you intend to use at night, plant some night-blooming nicotimea. Use daphne near an entryway and honeysuckle by the front gate.

Texture

Fine textures such as lawns, moss, and large smooth pavements tend to ac-centuate the mass and shape of the ground form itself and to increase its apparent size. They often act as a neutral screen or background for other textural elements placed on them—furnishings, sculpture, and people.

Coarse textures such as cobbles, bricks, tufty grass, herringbone decking, and redwood blocks or rounds call attention to the surface itself. For this reason, you should consider what texture range you are going to use to downplay the form of the topography or highlight it.

In dealing with textures, as with all other design criteria, be clear in your intentions. Use coarse or fine textures, and materials of strong color definition sparingly and dynamically. Avoid mixing too many textures in a single pavement area, but do distinguish special intricacies or use areas with textures and textural contrasts. Remember that fine-textured plants will lose their special quality if they are planted in the distant ground. Similarly, coarse-textured plants may be too bold for close-up viewing. For the best effect, place various textured plants where their qualities will be spotlighted.

In a patio, an area intended for barbecuing might be surfaced with smooth concrete (which is easily cleaned) while the remainder of the patio could have an exposed aggregate surface and thus be less reflective of light or more visually formal in keeping with use as a "living room."

When you plan for plants with fragrant foliage or flowers, be sure to place them where you can enjoy them most: next to the front door, outside a bedroom window, or along a garden path.

Plants with striking textures function as accents in the landscape. When they are used sparingly and combined with other less dynamic plants, they can be the focal point of the garden.

These plants with small, finely-cut foliage offer close up textural interest, especially in combination with the pale stones. From a distance, however, fine-textured plants have a neutral quality.

Every texture influences the overall feeling in your landscape, so your choices should be made with care. Coarsely textured materials, like the stones set in concrete (left), would not be a good choice for a barbecue area. The smooth brick pattern (above) has just the right texture for formal outdoor living areas, and the lacy ferns enhance the effect. Even shade patterns (right) can have a textural quality. The dappled light complements the adjacent stone mulch.

PLANTS, MATERIALS AND POSSIBILITIES

Selecting the colors, textures and materials is half the fun of creating your own landscape. With plants, wood, masonry, and other readily available materials, the possibilities are endless.

Landscapes are constructed from a variety of living and nonliving materials. Most people are familiar with the characteristics of nonliving construction materials —wood, stone, concrete, brick, etc.—and can make confident decisions to use one or the other based on appearance, suitability, and cost. But because of the diversity and immense selection, some people feel less confident about choosing the plants needed to complete their landscape.

A good, thoughtful design, and sensitive plant selection are the two most important aspects of creating a successful landscape. Because there isn't enough room in any one book to explain everything you need to know to select plants, it will be very helpful for you to use other sources, as well.

The more familiar you are with the plants that grow in your area, the better you will be able to create a beautiful landscape. Take note of the plants that appeal to you in other gardens. If you don't know their names, ask the owner, or take a small leaf sample to your local nursery or garden center.

Find out everything you can about the plants you like—their water, soil, fertilizer, and climate requirements, their natural form, the mature height and width, whether they have an invasive root system, if they lose their leaves or drop fruit, whether they provide dense or filtered shade, or any other characteristic that might be important in your particular situation.

Gardening books provide a wealth of information on a wide variety of plants. Many are like miniature encyclopedias that are extremely handy for plant selection. There are many books in the Ortho series that will help you become familiar with all types of plant material. Some of them are: *The World of Trees, How to Select & Care for Shrubs & Hedges, All About Ground Covers, Gardening with Color, All About Roses,* and *The World of Cactus and Succulents.*

For more detailed information concerning the construction of fences, decks, patios, walkways, and other garden projects, you can use the Ortho books: *How to Design & Build Decks & Patios, Garden Construction Know-How,* and *Wood Projects for the Garden.*

In addition to the materials you bring in from the outside, there are important elements that already exist in your landscape: the view from over the fence, the contours of the terrain, a mature tree, a large outcropping of rocks, or any other element that gives your landscape character.

If you have recently moved into a previously owned home, especially an older one, what is available for use in the landscape may not be readily apparent. The best advice in such cases is not to make any rash changes in the garden for at least a year. Most new homeowners discover that they have at least a year's worth of work to do on the inside of the house, anyway. Meanwhile, keep a close watch on the garden to see what surprises it reveals, and which of them you want to incorporate into your plan.

If you start remodeling the garden right away, particularly if you do so during the dormant season, you may discover, too late, that you've destroyed a 20-year-old bed of violets, peonies, or lilies of the valley. You may have ignored a dormant bed of nasturtiums that springs into vibrant life each year, or a thick tangle of branches that becomes a heavenly mass of lilac blossoms. These are special elements that cannot always be easily duplicated. In almost every case, their size or established nature make them a valued addition to the landscape.

Appropriate plants

One of the most important—and most often overlooked—aspects of choosing plant material is determining whether a plant is *appropriate* or not. For any particular spot there may be many appropriate choices; it all depends on how well the

A pleasing variety of plants and construction materials make the best landscapes.

The plants available for making a landscape are as diverse as they are plentiful. This planting shows many possible combinations.

FLOORS FOR THE LANDSCAPE

plant fits your requirements and how well it complements the landscape as a whole. For example, you may like the look of an Arizona cypress or dracaena palm, but both may look out of place in an area predominately planted with deciduous trees and broadleaf evergreens. Moreover, the climatic conditions in your landscape may be less than optimum for these choices.

The object in choosing plants for a landscape is to create a *willing garden.* Above all, use plants that you like—their flowers, form, fall color or whatever—but make sure they are plants well-suited to your individual environment.

As you look around at landscapes, it is much easier to find examples of inappropriate plant use than examples of appropriate use. The residence that unnecessarily cuts itself off from "borrowed views" with a planting of trees along the property line, where none was really necessary, does nothing but reinforce the smallness of the property; the tropical plants kept alive with tents and heaters during the yearly cold spell (plants that should be in a greenhouse, but are left out to suffer in the alien cold); the lawn that is never used for play or sitting, but must still be watered, fertilized, mowed and raked; the fast-growing property line hedge that has the function of separating neighboring planting beds—beds that would look much better from both sides if they were combined and planted in one theme; the giant forest tree planted to the south side of the patio or pool where it provides evermore shade as it grows, just where you want the most sun; the fruit tree that drops its rotting fruit on the entry path where they are easy to slip on; the seasonally unsightly vegetable garden or rose bed that sits in the everyday path where you can't help but notice how bad it looks in the off-season; the water-loving plants under the drought-loving tree that is failing because you can't help but overwater it; the monotonous use of a common palette of plants or the spotty and weak use of too many different plants, paving materials and forms, all out of balance . . . and the list goes on.

The definition of an appropriate plant is one that will be able to grow to maturity just where you plant it, with a minimum amount of effort on the part of the gardener. Appropriate plants fit into the overall landscape, and fit the needs and desires of the owner.

Materials for making landscapes

Since most people find it easy to think of outdoor space in terms of interior space, we have broken down the discussion on materials into these categories: "floors," including steps and walkways, "ceilings," and "walls" and "partial walls."

The first thing to choose in your landscape design should be the "carpeting" for your outdoor "rooms." The color, texture, and pattern of a good "floor" covering should blend with the other elements in the landscape. You can choose your material for easy maintenance as well, but, above all, it should be attractive.

Living choices

Of the many living possibilities for use as ground carpeting, *grass lawns* have been the favorite of generations of gardeners. A carpet of even, closely clipped greenery does more than just provide a level surface on which to play, eat, or just gaze down upon. A lawn may act as a unifying element, tying many different aspects of the garden together, simulating a mountain meadow. In summer drought areas, where mountain meadows never existed, consider lawn alternatives to save maintenance and water.

When *low, shrublike plants,* such as cotoneaster and wild lilac, are used as ground carpeting, they produce a less tailored look. Some other good choices include lilac, ivy, pachysandra, star jasmine, blue fescue, dusty miller, sedum, asparagus fern, mounding bougainvillea, bergenia, ferns, and naturalized wildflowers.

When you plant *ground covers,* remember that in its natural state the ground surface is rarely completely covered with vegetation, but is composed of a mosaic of free-form masses of colonies of the various plants that make up the plant community. Basic components of natural ground covers are rock outcroppings, boulders, or merely open patches of exposed soil. Once

When considering living choices for covering the ground, the most important decision to make is whether or not the area will receive much foot traffic. Particularly tender plants, such as the Baby's tears pictured above are attractive to look at but require distinct garden paths to avoid being damaged.

Floor coverings can be colorful, too. These gazanias put on a more or less constant show during the warm season. A few outcroppings of rock add interest to the otherwise even appearance.

Wooden decks have the distinct advantage of being able to create a level surface over an unlevel terrain. The natural quality of the material blends in well with almost any style of landscape.

A ground covering of rocks or gravel is generally a permanent addition to the landscape. The low cost, ease of installation, and ability to withstand a lot of wear give them many advantages.

they are well established, ground covers help to keep out weeds and can act as barriers. They can also add pleasing color, form, fragrance, and contrast.

Lawns in particular, and ground covers next, require some upkeep throughout the year. If low maintenance is what you are after, choose a hardy variety, and consider humanmade materials as well.

Nonliving materials

Keep in mind that solid, nonliving surfaces require good drainage; some, like untextured concrete, can be slippery when wet. Because solid surfaces can cut off the air supply to the soil, they should not be laid too close to the trunks of trees or large shrubs.

Gravel is an important material for "instant" landscaping and can provide immediate, inexpensive flooring in your garden.

It can have an informal look, or be formal and austere, as in the style of the French garden with its long, narrow, gravel-filled paths. Gravel is easy to put in, but it takes more or less constant upkeep with a rake to keep it free of leaves, twigs, and other garden debris. To help gravel stay in place, you can construct raised boundaries around it, made of 2-by-4-inch lumber, brick, or other materials. Another alternative is to set the gravel in asphalt that has been laid over sterilized soil, creating a composite by rolling the gravel into the asphalt. Weed seeds will not germinate in sterilized soil, thus eliminating the problem of weeds poking up through the combined asphalt and gravel.

Concrete slabs for use as patios are popular, practical, adaptable, and the most economical of all paved surfaces. Concrete can be cold and uninteresting if it is not relieved by some contrasting materials.

Popular ways to add color and texture to concrete are to inlay it with stone, intersperse concrete flooring with planter beds, and make geometric patterns out of concrete, brick and wood.

Wood is most often thought of in relation to making decks. At current prices, a wooden deck is about twice as expensive as concrete. But decks, unlike concrete or brick patios, are not limited to being built on level land, thus making it possible to place them just about anywhere that's appropriate. It's a good idea to keep your deck, the steps leading to and from it, and the surrounding walks related in some way. You can do this by making wood your motif. Perhaps you'll want to use railroad ties for steps and tree rounds for walkways.

To learn in detail about deck planning and construction and about concrete and other types of patios, see Ortho's *How to Design & Build Decks & Patios.*

The different effects given by these flooring materials demonstrate how important just this one choice is to your overall landscape plan. From top left to right: exposed aggregate concrete, flagstone used as coping around a pool, used bricks laid in a herringbone pattern, new bricks in the basketweave pattern, unglazed tiles, and cobblestones in a circular pattern.

Stones are another choice for an outdoor floor, although they are somewhat unkind to bare feet. When stones are laid in a bed of sand, their color and texture definitely add interest to the landscape. This method of flooring can be incorporated around trees and large shrubs, because air and water can circulate through the sand base. Selected stones are more expensive than either gravel or concrete.

Tiles can be used for a terrace or patio, especially in a Mediterranean-style garden. The tiles should be unglazed, because glazed tiles are extremely slippery when wet. Clay tiles blend in with both rustic and formal landscapes. However, concrete tiles, even when installed in an interesting pattern, are more easily laid than clay tiles. Clay tiles have to be carefully laid on a cement bed, over absolutely level terrain, and then mortared together, whereas concrete tiles can simply be laid in a

level bed of gravel and sand.

Bricks can be incorporated into the garden either as a formal, solid "rug" or informally in an end-to-side, zigzag pattern. A house does not need to be made of brick for a brick walkway or patio to look attractive close by. With their shape, color, and textural interest, bricks can calmly unify almost any garden. Bricks can be laid successfully and easily over a level bed of sand.

Bear in mind that many nonliving landscaping materials *recycle* well. Broken pieces of cement make good retaining walls or stepping stones. Even a patio can be devised out of such pieces, laying them in sand with 2-inch spaces between them, in which chamomile or creeping thyme is planted. Weathered fencing or shed boards also recycle well, if they do not look too unkempt. Their weathered look adds a softening effect to new construction. Old bricks

Above: Neutral colored stepping stones and gravel were used to complement this weathered wooden entrance way. Although the two materials are radically dissimilar, they make a pleasing combination. Above right: This unglazed **tile entrance contrasts with the wooden exterior of the house. The series of potted plants continues the terra cotta theme. Right: This unusual and useful combination of retaining wall and brick stairway adds interest to the patio.**

are invaluable assets, for their look of order without rigidity.

Steps and walkways can be made of any nonliving outdoor flooring material. Ideally, they should be made of materials that complement those used elsewhere in the landscape. If you have a brick terrace, you might want to use brick to edge concrete steps and paths. A walkway adjoining a cement patio might look best with an exposed aggregate surface, or perhaps something as simple as gray gravel.

To avoid creating an overwhelming effect, do not use too much of the same material throughout the landscape. On the other hand, to avoid visual confusion, don't mix too many unrelated materials in the same area. Whether you use only a few materials with a distinct contrast, or a greater number of closely related materials, the key word is balance. The overall scene should be harmonious.

CEILINGS FOR THE LANDSCAPE

Usually the most beautiful "ceiling" for outdoor rooms is the sky, whether it's blue, mottled with clouds, or overcast. While most outdoor space is open to the elements, it's almost always desirable for there to be a place in the landscape that's protected from the effects of sun, rain, and wind.

Trees

When asked to come up with ideas for ceilings in the garden, most people immediately think of a canopy of leaves from a large, overhanging tree. Trees can provide cooling protection from the sun, while at the same time mesmerizing us with their size and textures and the ever-changing patterns of their leaves.

Trees are woody plants that generally have only one stem or trunk and that generally grow to more than 15 feet high when mature. In selecting new trees or analyzing mature ones in your landscape, you should know the habits of the trees in question: their mature height, spread, form, texture, color, leaf fall and winter appearance, flowers, fragrance, fruit, rate of growth, hardiness, pest problems, potential life span, transplanting and pruning requirements, and any other special maintenance information.

The most satisfactory trees are those that will thrive in the natural conditions of your yard. If ease of maintenance is important to you, limit yourself to those species that adapt best to your particular site and that answer your specific design requirements.

Broad-leafed evergreens are trees that retain their leaves the year around, losing a percentage of them seasonally, but never all of them at one time. Examples are: the olive, pittosporum, live oak, eucalyptus, plumeria, acacia, tamarix, camphor, and magnolia. Individual species may have special features that you will want to note, such as flowers, fragrance, fruit, or particularly interesting form.

Coniferous trees are woody plants with scaly or needlelike leaves that bear cones of one type or another. This group includes the redwood, pine, juniper, yew, larch, fir, spruce, hemlock, arborvitae, cypress, and false cypress.

There are actually a few deciduous conifers, such as the dawn redwood from China and the southeastern bald cypress, but for the most part, conifers retain their foliage from 2 to 7 years, losing from ½ to ⅐ of the total each year. The major needle loss occurs in the fall months.

Deciduous trees are those that lose all or most of their leaves seasonally. Some of these species are only semideciduous in regions where it does not get cold enough to force them into full dormancy. This climatic factor often causes deciduous trees to perform less well in areas that don't have seasonally cold weather. For instance, the Chinese pistache will have better leaf color where there's a distinct cold snap in the fall than in warmer areas where fall weather comes on more gradually.

One of the most beautiful of all garden ceilings is a natural canopy of leaves. This enclosed garden in the Southwest has been made into an outdoor room with the addition of a grove of cottonwood trees.

A lattice overhead, painted a light color has a refined, formal effect. Lattice is easy to construct, and relatively inexpensive.

While canvas may not be the most durable of all outdoor ceilings, its crisp, traditional feeling cannot be matched.

Wooden overheads, with space left in between the slats, makes for a pleasing balance of light and shade. Such an open structure also allows for maximum air circulation.

Some examples of deciduous trees are the pin oak, walnut, aspen, apple, cherry, willow, ash, sycamore, elm, chestnut, and redbud. The special features presented by deciduous trees are their fall colors, their bare winter form, and their flowers, fragrance, and fruit. Deciduous trees provide summer shade, but also allow the winter sun to warm whatever lies beneath or behind them. This quality should be taken into consideration in many sites.

Trees that are native either to the *tropics* or to the *desert* are considered exotic in most regions of the country, and will grow willingly only in warm areas. Diversity abounds. Consider the date palm, tree fern, monkeypod, bunya-bunya, albizzia, joshua, banyon, cajeput, and ironwood.

When the climate allows for the use of these trees, they can form a lush tropical character or the feeling of a desert oasis, becoming interesting accents or making emphatic statements, like living sculptures in the landscape.

Plastic and fiberglass

For use in the garden, synthetic materials are usually less aesthetically pleasing than other natural materials. But translucent fiberglass or plastic panels overhead can ensure complete privacy from upstairs windows; soften the light; and when viewed from underneath, provide interesting patterns from overhanging tree limbs. The wooden struts over which the fiberglass or plastic is laid will also cast shadow patterns on the floor. A synthetic ceiling has the advantage of providing an environment that's almost like a greenhouse, usually ideal for semitropical plants. But usually its greatest virtue lies in its economy.

Canvas

Canvas can create the festive air of a circus tent or the crisp good looks of a nautical scene. Natural light glows softly through it. As a bonus, you can dismantle and store it at the first signs of seasonal rain. When spring arrives, you simply relace the canvas to its frame. In windy areas, canvas can be used for side panels that act as windbreaks. A canvas shelter can also be made into an enchanting gazebo, and at less expense than one made of lath. In time, though, canvas will take its toll from the sun and the other elements, and it will need replacing.

Wood and reeds

The best of both sun and shade can be provided when an open area is designed adjacent to one that's sheltered overhead.

If you make the overhead structure solid, you'll have complete shade, but you'll also trap the warm air under the cover. In warm summer areas, a lack of ventilation may make the enclosure uninviting.

Rolls of bamboo screening, or wooden slats pitched tent fashion, filter the sunshine and provide interesting shadow effects on the ground surface underneath. A lattice has an effect that's similar to wooden slats, though more dramatic.

WALLS AND PARTIAL WALLS

To keep its even appearance, this unusual needled evergreen requires selective pruning rather than shearing. Hedges are among the most appropriate of all garden walls, providing a background for other plants.

A long row of espaliered evergreen pears makes a beautiful division between two properties. Espaliered plants take considerable time and effort, but the effect is dramatic.

Such a variety of outdoor "walls" and "partial walls" is possible that the only thing we can say they have in common is their verticalness. Outdoor walls can be formed out of trees, hedges, shrubs, solid brick, wood, or other materials. Hedge walls can be loose and billowy, giving them a casual look, or dense and tightly sheared for a more formal effect. Green walls are architecturally neutral, but are more romantic in spirit than solid walls, and are also less expensive and forbidding.

While partial walls may actually *be* permanent structures or plantings, they tend to have an airier and lighter look about them. Partial walls are often made to be versatile: such as shades which can be rolled down, foot by foot, for protection from the sun's glare, then rolled up again for an unadulterated view; to be moved here and there where privacy is desired, then to be removed completely when it's time to socialize.

Shrubs

Shrubs, like trees, are woody plants. In general, shrubs have more than one stem or trunk, and are smaller than 15 feet when mature. The distinction between small trees and large shrubs is not hard and fast, and often the two terms are used interchangeably when referring to plants that fit this description. Shrubs, like trees, are also broad-leafed and coniferous evergreens, deciduous, and exotic.

Broad-leafed evergreen shrubs include: the firethorn, rhododendron, abelia, camellia, poinsettia, acuba, bottlebrush, boxwood, privet, and crape myrtle. Broad-leafed evergreen shrubs are among the most versatile plants in the landscape: They can be used for enclosures, screens, and barriers, and are often notable for their form, fragrance, color, and fruit.

Deciduous shrub examples are the forsythia, redbud, quince, dogwood, hazelnut, sumac, rose, lilac, hydrangea, and elderberry. In cold climates, deciduous shrubs can make excellent texture and color contrasts when massed with evergreen shrubs.

Coniferous shrubs include the juniper, yew, Japanese black pine, weeping blue spruce, and dwarf or semidwarf forms of coniferous trees.

Examples of *tropical* and *desert*

Luxuriant growing vines, such as this bougainvillea, have the ability to soften the most geometric structures.

Top: With a minimum amount of pruning, a vine can be made to have the delicate effect of a tracery against a solid wall. Above: Vines can also be made to cover a vertical surface completely, giving an appearance similar to a hedge.

shrubs are the Chinese hybiscus, fatsia, fuchsia, plumago, jasmine, gardenia, mock orange, oleander, natal plum, and sweet olive.

Shrubs can serve as walls in your outdoor rooms without being planted too closely together and left unsheared. They can be evergreen or deciduous, and may flower or not. You might decide on a deciduous variety if you want a tall shrub to screen an undesirable view. When it loses its leaves in the winter, it will still provide some screening and allow the low, winter sun to play over that part of your garden that otherwise might not get much natural light. The bare skeletons of shrubs in the winter can be sculptural and pleasing to look at.

Vines

Vines are extremely versatile plants. Besides creeping, trailing, crawling, and climbing, they quickly bring color and fragrance, and richness and variety to any outdoor setting. Some vines, such as bougainvillea, also make good ground covers. Vines will soften the effect of a fence or any solid structure and can themselves make living walls or screens.

A climbing rose, such as 'Lady Banks', makes a charming, loose, informal wall. A clinging vine, such as creeping fig, can "wallpaper" itself to your fence or the back of your garage, and become a neat, crisp, flat covering that provides an evenly textured mat of green. Clematis vines, although deciduous, offer some of the most beautiful blossoms possible. Jasmines are popular vines, and many varieties add a wonderful scent to the garden, along with the beauty of their flowers. The bounteous blooms of wisteria, the most romantic of all vines, can hang over the top of a fence or garland a wall. Before choosing a vine, though, make sure that it is not overly invasive or so fast-growing as to cause problems later.

Vines have several methods for holding on to vertical surfaces: *discs* or *suction cups* (Virginia creeper), *aerial roots* (philodendron), *twining stems*, in which the leaders actually grow around the supports (wisteria), *tendril coils* (passafloria), *leaf-stalk coils* (nasturtium), and *thorns* (climbing roses and berries). Many other plants can be artificially supported to give the effect of vines by affixing them to upright stakes and other vertical surfaces.

Screens

An inexpensive *reed* screen, available in a roll, can be quickly erected to make an effective partial wall in an "instant" landscape. It is flexible and easy to work with. Generally, this kind of screening lends itself to an informal setting, but it can also blend into a small, formal oriental garden. Reed screening will need replacing every two or three years.

Cement blocks

More expensive and permanent than reed screening is a wall or partial wall made of cement blocks. The variety of geometrical openwork they offer can be combined into patterned walls that assure both privacy and air circulation. One or two carefully chosen patterns can be used by themselves or in combination with solid blocks. To be certain of the solidity and permanence of your wall of cement blocks, set them in mortar.

Trellises

Perhaps the most handsome humanmade screens are trellises. Traditionally, trellises are used in formal French gardens, but they can also have a modern or rustic effect, depending on the pattern that's chosen and whether or not the wood is rough or finished. Trellising can create a feeling of enclosure or privacy without blocking the sun and breeze or totally eliminating the view. Trellis patterns can also add vertical or horizontal interest. Some of the most attractive trellises are those that are partially covered with vines.

Fences

Fences provide privacy, support vines, protect against strong winds, create comfortably warm spots in sunny areas, add horizontal or vertical interest, and can unify a house and garden when made of a material that harmonizes with the house.

Steel: If you want everlasting security, erect a chain link fence, but disguise it with vines or a hedge, or make it "disappear" by painting it a dark, natural color. A fence should be as attractive on one side as the other, so before constructing any type of fence, you should consult your neighbor.

Wood: If your house is constructed in a Colonial style, by all means construct a picket fence. These and some other style can be bought in readymade sections; the more elaborate Williamsburg picket fences are handmade.

If your house has clapboard siding, a fence made of this material and constructed in the same manner is a good choice and can be painted the same color as the house. Soften the long, horizontal lines of a clapboard fence with random plantings of a variety of shrubs, vines, or trees.

Large lumber yards usually display short sections of a variety of wooden fence styles.

Iron: If your house has a formal French style or is a Victorian gingerbread, you may want to sacrifice the privacy of a solid fence for the security and good looks of an ornamental wrought-iron fence.

Brick: If your house is made of brick, you may want to place brick pillars at strategic intervals and join them with iron or wood in an open pattern, rather than imprisoning yourself within walls of solid brick.

The combination of solid rock and delicate, colorful plants has a very special quality that makes a rock wall, such as this one, particularly beautiful. Rock walls can be constructed from materials found on your property, broken pieces of concrete, or stones imported from another site.

A fence is not just a fence. The wide variety of available materials allows you to achieve many very different effects. From top left to right: Lath lattice on top of a solid fence, open form fretwork, shingled fence, fence with Oriental motif, simple rustic fence, solid stone wall, formal white lattice pattern, diagonally placed boards for partial view, and open fencing with maximum privacy.

ACCENTS IN THE LANDSCAPE

Succulents have some of the most unusual forms of any plants. They make unique accent plantings, especially when several species are combined for a contrasting effect.

The medium-sized Japanese maple (*Acer palmatum*) is a favorite for use as an accent tree. Its intricately cut foliage makes it one of the most beautiful of all specimens.

Plants, and other elements in the landscape, do not always fall neatly into the structural categories of floors, ceilings, and walls. Accents are often features such as specimen plants or sculptures.

Accent plants are especially selected for their fine or unusual features. Accent plants usually look the most attractive when they are planted together, in small groups or in masses.

Plan your use of accent plantings carefully. Too many different accents in a small area may make it look like a botanical garden or nursery, instead of a well-designed landscape. Try planting them in masses, so that their color, form, or whatever makes them unique will really have center stage. If you use an accent alone, set it off with simpler vegetation around it.

If you have to decide between understatement and overkill, it's wise to choose understatement. If a section of your yard is planted with just one type of shrub, strikingly contrasting plants may be just the effect that's needed. But, if four or five different shrubs with different color, texture,

and form are planted in the same area, be cautious about adding accent plants there —you may cause visual overkill.

When accent plants are massed together, even when there are a number of varieties, they can make an oasis. See page 22 for the oasis landscaping style. To achieve the best effect, an oasis should contrast with extreme simplicity. The typical oasis in nature is surrounded by flat, sandy areas, but this simplicity can also be achieved with mosses or other small-textured plants. Cacti and other succulents make excellent oasis landscapes.

Cacti and other succulents

The many forms of succulents, including the cactus, are striking when they are positioned appropriately. Their bizarre shapes and colors make them a group that deserves special attention. These desert plants have come in and gone out of favor three times in the United States since the 1880s. They are currently in vogue to stay, we hope. Examples of cacti and other succulents are the echeveria, lapideria,

Christmas cactus, agave, aloe, yucca, crassula, euphorbia, sedum, and dudlea. For more about how to grow them and use them as landscaping subjects, see Ortho's book, *The World of Cactus and Succulents*.

Annuals, biennials, and perennials

While annuals, biennials, and perennials are plants of great diversity, they are grown primarily for their colorful flowers in many forms.

An annual is a plant that grows from seed to maturity in one year and then dies. In choosing where and when to use annuals, remember that they need yearly replanting and the constant care that new plants require. Because of their ephemeral quality, they make excellent container plants. Be sure to put annuals where they will make a dramatic impact from their splashes of color, strong fragrances, and fast-growing forms. In areas with mild climates, it's possible to rotate annual plantings so that there is something interesting and colorful in the garden in almost every season.

Annuals provide a quick-growing display of color wherever you need it the most. Because they can be changed with the season, they are ideal accent plants.

Perennials (shown here are peonies and delphiniums) have a wide variety of forms and colors. Most live from year to year, making a permanent addition to the landscape.

The difference between biennials and perennials is that biennials take two seasons to grow to maturity, while perennials take three seasons, and sometimes longer. Since biennials and perennials represent more permanent plantings, it's important to organize the way they are laid out rather carefully. They are tremendously varied in form, size, and cultural requirements, making them favorites in "gardeners' gardens." The classic style of perennial borders has been refined over the years into a gardening art; these borders are featured in English country gardens (see page 16).

Bulbs

Bulbs are plants that have fleshy or enlarged roots. Unlike other plants, they use their underground roots to store food during the dormant period. Corms, tubers, tuberous roots, and rhyzomes also fall under this definition. Most of them blossom from 12 to 26 weeks after they are planted. This waiting period makes it a surprise and a delight when they begin to come up.

Bulbs include daffodils, tulips, and narcissus. Corms include freesias and gladiolas. Tubers include gloxinias, tuberous begonias, and anemone. Tuberous roots include dahlias and ranunculus. Rhyzomous plants include wild strawberry and canna.

Fungi

Tree and ground mosses, lichens, mushrooms, and other forms of fungi should not be overlooked as part of a landscape planting. Use these unique plants where they will add a special bit of interest.

A famous garden in Kyoto, Japan features numerous varieties of mosses. Rock outcroppings in many natural areas are covered with colorful lichens. Clusters of mushrooms, although not always edible, are certainly fun to come across in a garden. The Spanish moss of the deep South hangs from trees in wild and hoary threads, contributing greatly to the atmosphere of that region. The mistletoe that grows in many oak and walnut trees, although not healthy for the trees, adds its own statement to the landscape.

Vegetables

Vegetables can be striking additions to the landscape. Ornamental cabbage (sometimes called kale) is handsome as a ground cover or annual border. Corn and sunflowers can act as accents or bold barriers. Peas and beans are quick-growing annual vines. Swiss chard provides outstanding color. And artichokes offer a perennial contrast in texture and color. Besides making unusual ornamentals, vegetable plants have the bonus of their harvest, freely given.

Berries

Berry vines are a delightful group of plants that have several distinct uses. As a group, they make good barriers, as well as mounding ground covers. Wild blackberries are seen by many as the scourge of the garden, but when left alone to do what they will, they can be very attractive, provided you can give them the space they need.

This mass planting of ornamental cabbage shows how vegetables can be used as accents in the landscape. Fast-growing and temporary, they can be changed from year to year.

Even though they are traditionally planted with the rest of the food plants, these red currants are about as ornamental as possible. Their shiny red fruit makes an unusual summer accent.

Structural accents

Not all accents are plants. Some of the most time-honored accents in the landscape are humanmade: garden pools, pergolas and arbors, gazebos, ornamental containers, sculpture, and garden furniture are among the most common.

As with accent plants, structural accents should be used with restraint. A pair of ornamental containers, a solitary garden pool, or one gazebo is usually all a landscape can handle without becoming confused. Not all landscapes require an accent, but if you decide to use one, be sure to place it so that it receives the attention it deserves.

Before adding any structural accents, consider the style of your landscape. Because of their prominence, these accents should be chosen with a careful eye for appropriateness and authenticity.

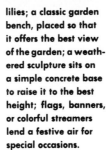

Structural, and other non-living accents can take many forms. For the strongest effect, place them where they will receive the most attention and use them sparingly. Clockwise, from the top: A formal pond, complete with goldfish and water lilies; a classic garden bench, placed so that it offers the best view of the garden; a weathered sculpture sits on a simple concrete base to raise it to the best height; flags, banners, or colorful streamers lend a festive air for special occasions.

THE DESIGN PROCESS

Making a plan is the all-important step in landscaping. While the plan is still on paper, you can change your mind as much as you want without wasting a nickel. No matter how sketchy or professional your drawing is, a plan will save you both time and money.

The materials and tools needed to produce professional working drawings may not be as extensive—or expensive—as you think. Everything you need is shown in the photograph at left. See page 60 for the list of supplies.

Making a plan for a landscape is really a form of shorthand—an easy and effective way of notating ideas. In fact, you cannot make a workable design without a plan. As you record, study, and improve your ideas, the design develops. You may find yourself making notes, scrutinizing pictures of other landscapes, and making drawings of your own original ideas. All these are intermediate steps to finding a design solution. The more possibilities you think out, the closer you are to an effective design.

You can draw your landscape design either freehand or with the aid of mechanical drafting tools. Whichever method you choose, you still will need to scale your plan. Scaling ensures accuracy when you are figuring how much you'll need of soil amendments, ground cover plants, trees, shrubs, and so forth.

Architect's scale. One very helpful tool is the architect's scale. It calibrates dimensions directly into whatever scale you want to use. For example, if you are using a scale where ¼ inch equals 1 foot, the architect's scale would represent a 7-foot length as 1¾ inch. Even if you plan to draw your entire plan freehand, invest in this tool—it will save you many times its cost in time and effort.

Drawing methods and supplies

As we mentioned, you can draw your base plan freehand or with the help of mechanical drafting tools. There are many aspects of a landscape plan that can be successfully drawn freehand, but certain drafting tools, such as triangles and circle templates, will help you make uniform angles and circles.

Choose a *circle template* that can draw circles from ½ to 3 inches in diameter. This tool is very useful for laying out planting and irrigation systems. Even if your landscape has no circular details at all, it still will help you draw circles to symbolize forms—for example, to represent the approximate spread of a particular plant. (This approximation is based on the plant's anticipated mature spread. This method offers the easiest way to determine how many shrubs or trees you'll need to make a mass planting. To find out the number of ground cover plants you'd need in a given area, take the square footage of the area and divide it by the footage requirement of each variety of ground cover.)

You'll also need *graph paper*. Attach it to a flat table, holding it in place with *drafting tape*. This differs from masking tape in that it comes off easily without tearing the paper. Be sure the graph paper is lined to the scale you intend to use—for example, if your plan uses ¼ inch to represent 1 foot, buy graph paper with ¼-inch squares. It can be very distracting if the paper is lined to a different scale than the one you are using. Graph paper is avail-

An architect's scale is simple to use, and is a helpful tool for anyone designing and planning a landscape. To keep the plan in scale, consider purchasing one, even if you intend to draw all your plans freehand.

able in various scales at most art supply stores. There, you can also get *tracing paper* to use over the base plan for experimental drawings. Tracing paper comes in rolls as well as sheets. Your best buy is a 12-or 14-inch roll of yellow or white *flimsey*—a thin tracing paper that is ideal for quick overlays and sketches.

For early freehand sketches, a *soft lead pencil*, one marked B or F, is best. Harder pencils, such as H or 2H, make finer lines and are more suitable for fine-line drafting on working drawings.

As you draft plans, don't get too entranced by the drafting equipment. Triangles, templates, and so on can be very helpful tools, but they shouldn't overly influence your design.

As you move closer to the working-drawing stage, you may want to use more technical drafting tools, including a drafting board and T-square. These tools can help you produce professional-looking drawings; but remember that the purpose of mechanical drafting is to make lines that indicate well-defined thoughts. It's like typing: If you don't know how to spell, typing will make that fact more evident than handwriting will.

Basic equipment
If you do plan to do a detailed design with professional drafting tools, purchase the following equipment:

Pad of 18″ x 24″ 1000H tracing paper
Roll of 12″ of 14″ flimsey sketching paper
Transparent 6″, 45° triangle
Small template
Compass
Flat architect's scale
Roll of drafting tape
24″ x 36″ drafting board
36″ T-square
Lead pointer
Artgum eraser
Eagle drafting pencil (soft)
Lead holder with one box of H leads
Eraser shield

Whether you've taken a drafting class or have never learned the skill formally, you can make very satisfactory drawings with just the basic equipment and a little practice. You may find that your interest in drafting grows more than you anticipated. If so, go with it—the more thought-out and detailed your landscaping plan is, the easier it will be to carry out the actual construction.

Before you begin to plan and design in earnest, you need to know as much exact information about the site as possible. Get as clear a picture of it as you can and then transfer the information to paper: Consider the site's size, existing plantings, walkways, fences, walls, slopes, out-buildings, and any other significant characteristics.

THE BASE PLAN

Just walking around your property will show you what you've got thus far; but creating a new landscape requires translating your three-dimensional landscape into two dimensions—in short, you need to make a drawing of your *base plan*. This piece of paper will be an invaluable aid; not only will it help you get familiar with the details of your current landscape and make their relationships clear, but it will also enhance your ability to visualize any changes and additions you'd like to make.

If you already have a base plan of your site (obtained from your builder, a former owner, or the city building department), you can use it instead of drawing your own. However, you still will have to do three things: (1) make sure that it is drawn correctly; (2) make sure that whatever is indicated on the plan is still part of your landscape; and (3) incorporate any new objects or plantings into the plan.

Making a base plan has additional benefits: the task of measuring the site will probably take you into corners of your yard that you rarely visit. Often, the remotest areas of a site offer the most striking and seldom seen views, exaggerate the size of the lot, or offer the viewer a certain amount of peace and solitude not available in the more travelled parts of the landscape. As you explore these areas, keep your mind open for the best ways to capitalize on their unique qualities.

If you have no base plan, you'll need to make your own from scratch. The following pages will tell you how to do this.

Scale
To determine which scale to choose for your plan, consider the information you want to portray. If you are working with a space that's very small but has many details, choose a large scale, such as 1 inch to the foot. But if your site is very large, you may need to use a scale of 1 inch to 20 feet in order to fit the entire site onto a single sheet of paper. (Of course, you can use larger scale instead, and split the site up, covering only part of it on each sheet.) Indicate the scale somewhere on the plan itself (for example, put down "¼ inch = 1 foot").

To depict the normal residential landscape (½-acre lot or less), you usually can use ¼ inch to the foot (written as "1:4 scale")—in fact, this is the scale we recommend. (If you already have a good plan of your site, you can adjust it to a ¼-inch scale; simply measure and copy the plan onto another sheet.)

You'll need to have a datum, or *base line*. If your site is adjacent to a building, you can use one of the walls. If your site is in the open, where there's no existing base line, you can use one edge of the property; or else you can use a string between two stakes to set up a straight line, and then measure the remainder of the site from your improvised base line.

In orienting the first wall line on the paper, make sure you leave enough room to draw in the entire site. Always draw the plan with north at the top or on the left side of the paper; this standard practice will help building inspectors and others reading your plan orient themselves to the site.

What to include in your plan
As you work across the landscape with a 50- or 100-foot tape measure, make note of the location of everything that seems important. Include any of the following fixed objects in your base plan: house walls; doors; windows; fences; shrubs; tree trunks and leaf canopies; existing irrigation; spigots; pools; paving and paths; overhead and underground utility lines; drainage courses; property lies; easements and setbacks; and shadow patterns of neighboring buildings.

Once you've recorded every significant detail on your base plan, get a clean sheet of paper and trace the plan onto that. The newer version will be more precise. Use the architect's scale to scale off dimensions; use triangles to check angles; and use a template or compass to draw true circles.

Now take this clean, accurate copy and go back to the site. Covering your clean copy with an overlay, note the following information: Views (both good and bad); buildings and other objects; shadow patterns from large trees (deciduous tree shadows will change when the trees lose—and regrow—their leaves); sunny spots; direction of the prevailing wind; wind-free areas; areas where snow and rain runoff collect; and access points and circulation routes (note how they work—or fail to work).

Make a note of any trees or shrubs you want to remove, as well as those you want to save. Are there any lawn areas, ground covers, large rocks or other elements that will need to be removed to facilitate your new plans? If so, indicate their removal on the plan.

Before you can begin to design a landscape, you need to have a clear picture of the site and the existing conditions. Once this information has been transferred to paper, you have what is called a base plan. The first draft of the base plan can be somewhat sketchy, but after measuring the site and marking the location of every significant detail, you should re-draw it as neatly as possible. Once complete, it should look similar to the plan below.

Base plan

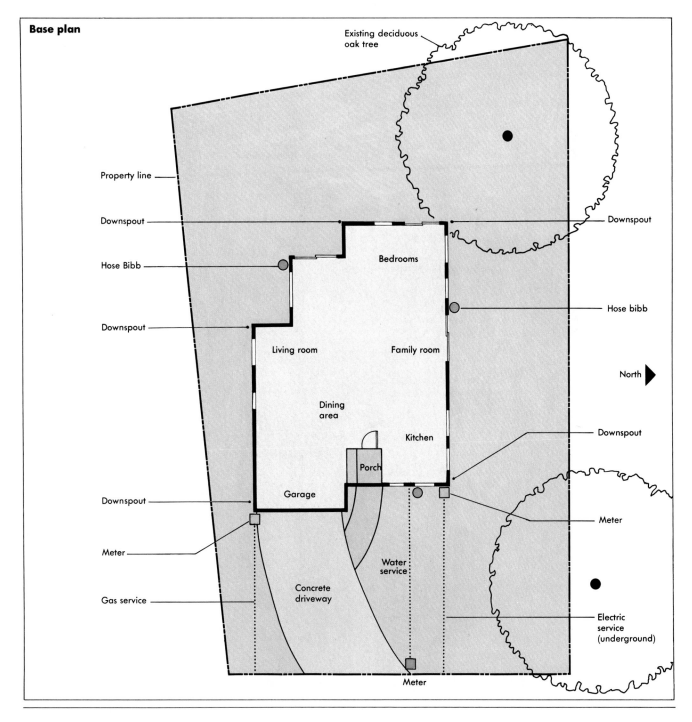

Existing deciduous oak tree

Property line

Downspout

Hose Bibb

Downspout

Downspout

Meter

Gas service

Bedrooms

Living room

Family room

Dining area

Kitchen

Porch

Garage

Concrete driveway

Water service

Downspout

Hose bibb

North

Downspout

Meter

Electric service (underground)

Meter

If you intend to alter a grade—either by removing it or increasing it—make a note of it on the plan. Drainage problems can affect the intended use of a particular space. If you have an area where water collects, and you'd like to locate a patio or some other use space there, be sure to read the sections on drainage in Chapter Six before planning any solutions. If you have to install drain tiles, this should be indicated on the plan. The location of retaining walls, their height, width and slope (if any) should also be noted. Details for constructing walls can be found on page 78.

Now is also the time to think about watering system. Because watering is such a primary consideration in any garden, planning a system is an important part of any landscape design. We have detailed such plans in Chapter Six on pages 82 to 89. Be sure to read this section when you come to this aspect of your design.

After all these drawings and redrawings, you may find that your base plan contains a confusing number of notes and arrows. For clarity's sake, you can make a tracing of just the basic lines of fixed forms, such as the house walls and the street curb, and work from them. But don't throw your marked-up base plan away; it may be messy, but it will help enormously when you get to the concept-drawing phase.

Seeing with fresh eyes

If you think you already know your property like you know the back of your hand, you may wonder what you could possibly learn that you don't know right now. But if you can put off the urge to hurry into construction, and instead give yourself time to develop a design, you may end up with a solution that's as unexpected as it is agreeable. Look at your site like a first-time visitor; don't let your preconceptions limit your design.

The best way to get an idea of the landscaping possibilities of your site is to familiarize yourself with the design concepts discussed in Chapter Three. Then you can develop some new ways of seeing your site. For example, what would the views to and from the areas you want to landscape be like at different elevations either above or below ground level? Can you connect the house to the garden with a deck, and thus create a better circulation pattern among them? How will a new deck or patio look from inside the house? from the street? Climb up a ladder to check out views from possible raised decks. Outline ground-level areas with water hoses or strings to get an idea of what they'd look like set off in one way or another. In general, broaden the limits of your site as much as you can; the better you know your site, the more easily new ideas will stream through your mind and onto paper.

Once you have the final version of your base plan, tape a piece of tracing paper over the plan and go back outdoors. Make a close inspection of the site, **looking for such details as: which views need screening, which views you would like to accentuate, the direction of the sun and the prevailing wind, etc. Don't** **worry if the results look messy; this information will be invaluable later in the design process.**

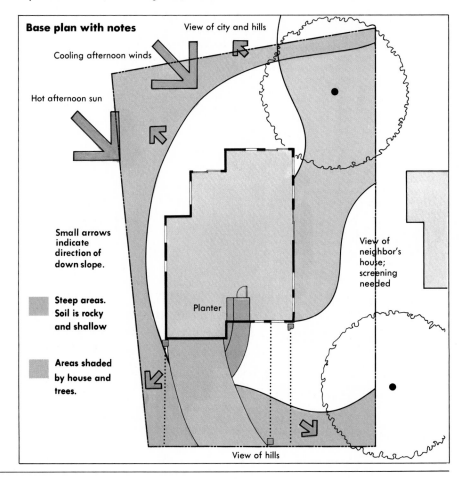

Base plan with notes

View of city and hills

Cooling afternoon winds

Hot afternoon sun

Small arrows indicate direction of down slope.

Steep areas. Soil is rocky and shallow

Areas shaded by house and trees.

Planter

View of neighbor's house; screening needed

View of hills

30 QUESTIONS

Once you have completed your base plan and made all the necessary notations, ask yourself some specific questions, using the following questions as a guide. They will help you evaluate the needs of the people who will be using the landscape, and to determine many characteristics of the site. In addition, just getting your thoughts down onto paper may clarify the site's potentials and stimulate a workable design.

1 What uses do you currently make of your garden and landscape?

2 What do you most like about your site?

3 What don't you like about the existing landscape?

4 What specific uses do you want to plan for?

5 How do you and other members of your family plan to use the landscape and its new spaces?

6 If you have children, what specific uses will they be growing into and out of?

7 If you have pets, do they have any specific requirements that will influence your design? For example, do you want to shut them out of or let them into specific areas?

8 If you were to think of various parts of your landscape as outdoor rooms or extensions of your indoor living spaces, what would you call them? Kitchen? storage? living room?

9 What is the architectural style of your house? What aspect of it do you want to carry through into the landscape?

10 Is there some particular landscape style that you want to use? For example, formal? Japanese? natural?

11 Are there any special plants you want to use?

12 What colors of foliage and flowers do you want to use?

13 Are you or any member of your family allergic to any plants or to bees?

14 What sort of paving surfaces do you like?

15 Does your site require any special screening to ensure privacy?

16 How do you feel about the look and feel of the entrance to your house?

17 What design ideas from Chapter Three would you like to include?

18 Do you have a special need or desire to save water? attract birds? screen the wind?

19 How much money have you budgeted for improvements?

20 How much time will you have to work on the project?

21 How much time will you have to maintain it once it is installed?

22 How long do you expect it to last before you have to do major remodeling again?

23 Are materials easily available? Are there any materials or objects you want to use to create a special feeling?

24 Are there any easements, setbacks, or other zoning regulations that will influence what you do?

25 Are there any underground utility lines or old water pipes you should be aware of? Can you locate them from old plans or by digging sample holes?

26 Will local building codes apply to any of your work?

27 Do any of your potential plans influence your neighbors' interests? If so, have you discussed your plans with them?

28 Are there any "Heritage Trees" (trees protected by local ordinances) or other special elements you should take into consideration?

29 Do you have the tools, patience, and skills to complete the project?

30 Are there any other considerations that will influence what you can do in making your landscape?

Even if you haven't been able to give complete answers, keep these questions in mind and return to them as you work into the concept-drawing phase. Knowing what you *don't* know can help you be on the lookout for the answers.

MAKING A PLAN—FROM CONCEPT TO WORKING DRAWINGS

Some people can conceptualize designs easily, but most people need time to find a good answer to a design problem. Happily, tracing paper is as inexpensive as it is indispensable. When you put tracing paper on top of your base plan, you can change your mind to your heart's content. This is the time to experiment with a variety of forms for the spaces, shrubs and tree masses, and various types of paved surfaces in your landscape. You can lay out rectangles, squares, circles, angles, and free-forms in many sizes and configurations, each on a separate overlay to see whether they appeal to you or not.

After working out several conceptual designs, choose one; it can be a version unto itself, or a combination of several overlays. During the concept phase, limit your attention to general uses and site considerations. Later on, during the working-drawing phase, you can refine your plan and select actual materials and dimensions.

The first step in making a concept drawing is to do several "bubble" plans on tracing paper laid over your base plan. With nothing more than sketchy circles—bubbles—indicate the specific areas you want to include in your final landscape (lawn areas, decks, play areas, etc.) and how you want them situated.

After using the bubble plans to determine the size of the basic space and the way they should be combined, refine the ideas with concept drawings. At the concept stage, however, you should still feel free to change your mind as often as you like. The final concept drawing should be fairly specific and accurate, containing the type of detailed information shown at right.

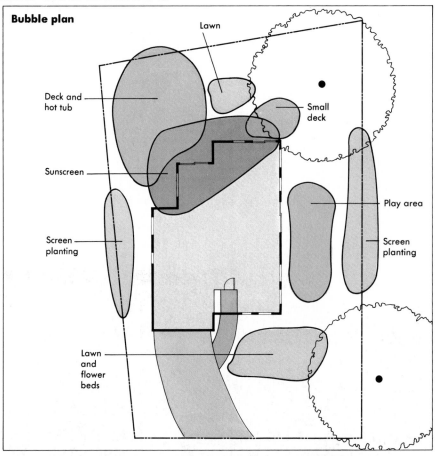

Bubble plan

Lawn

Deck and hot tub

Small deck

Sunscreen

Play area

Screen planting

Screen planting

Lawn and flower beds

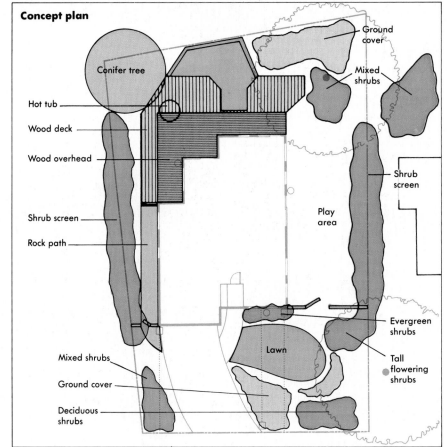

Concept plan

Ground cover

Conifer tree

Mixed shrubs

Hot tub

Wood deck

Wood overhead

Shrub screen

Shrub screen

Rock path

Play area

Evergreen shrubs

Mixed shrubs

Lawn

Tall flowering shrubs

Ground cover

Deciduous shrubs

Concept drawing, site plan

Your working drawing will be mere fool's gold if your concept drawing is no good. The purpose of the concept drawing is to figure out solutions to your particular landscaping needs. Use a concept drawing to get an idea of: How you want one space to relate to another; the size of the outdoor rooms; the connections and circulation between them; the views to and from the spaces; and special design considerations, such as sequence and the separation of public and private spaces. Concentrate on how you will use and move around within the spaces and what form the space will take. There are usually many good solutions to any design problem, not just one.

Once you know the separate spaces you want to include in your landscape, list them on your base plan (to scale), and assign them rough sizes. When determining what size to make your spaces, use the size of the equivalent indoor room as a touchstone. For example, if you want a space for outdoor dining and a barbeque, use the dimensions of a good-sized kitchen and dining alcove as a starting point. But don't make outdoor spaces (for instance, patios and decks) so large that they are uncomfortable and inconvenient; there's nothing pleasant about a patio that looks like half the guests never arrived for the party.

If your deck or patio will be used primarily for entertaining, think of how much space it takes to entertain the same number of people indoors, and whether more space will be required outdoors. Achieving a sense of intimacy outdoors happens when you relate the space's size to your needs and the human scale.

Bubble plan In drawing these early plans, make quick circles or bubbles to represent the spaces. The different sizes of the bubbles will indicate their respective uses and relative importance. A *bubble plan* will keep you from thinking about details at a time when you should be concentrating on the more general problems of space, size, and flow.

Another way of determining spaces for patios, decks, walks, and so forth is to draw them on different pieces of tracing paper, or cut them out of cardboard. Then move these pieces of paper around on the base plan, trying out different configurations. When you find a combination you like, trace it and put it aside to reconsider later on. Once you have developed several agreeable combinations, go back over each one and see whether it accomplishes your design goals.

As you arrange and draw your preliminary concept designs, keep in mind that you are creating space for activities—for instance, planting, contemplating, eating, relaxing, and socializing. Think of the real or ideal connections between these spaces, such as easy access from the barbeque to the kitchen, or from the hot tub to the bedroom or den. Be very conscious of circulation—where you will need to walk, and when you will want to be out of the walking area. The effective use of any room, indoors or out, may be reduced if it becomes simply a corridor from one place to another.

Draw sketch after sketch on tracing paper; save only those that seem to have the best points. Draw freehand, using the graph paper units as a guide to keep your experimental spaces roughly to scale. Most of all, be conscious of the basic form —the bubbles of space—and how well various designs create continuity and flow, and answer your needs.

Think about: Changing levels; raising an area aboveground with a deck; using planters or shrub masses; or leveling a hilly area for a patio. Consider: How the landscape will look from interior rooms; how you can incorporate existing elements; and what the orientation of the spaces are to the sun angle, views, noise, and winds. Go back and review the elements in Chapter Three and use them to strengthen your landscape plan.

Thumbnail sketches will help you evaluate your ideas, if you are still having trouble visualizing certain aspects of your design, by getting a different picture of them. They are usually very simple, often taking the form of a *bird's eye view*—a sketch drawn from an angle above the object. Other views to consider are sections and elevations.

Sections show a cut profile of an object. (For example, a section of a deck would show the railing, the surface of the deck, the joists, beams, posts, and footings.) Section drawings are good for studying how walls, seating, decking, or anything else with a vertical composition fits together in the design.

Elevations also express vertical composition, but instead of showing a cutaway view, they indicate what you see when you look at an object head-on, such as the front of your house. This type of picture is especially good for showing changes of materials.

Simple sketches of sections and elevations will help you formulate your own ideas and communicate them to other people. Many people who find it difficult to visualize a plan have no trouble at all when they look at a simple sketch.

Before you proceed to your working drawing, estimate the costs of your plans. Guidelines for this are on page 68.

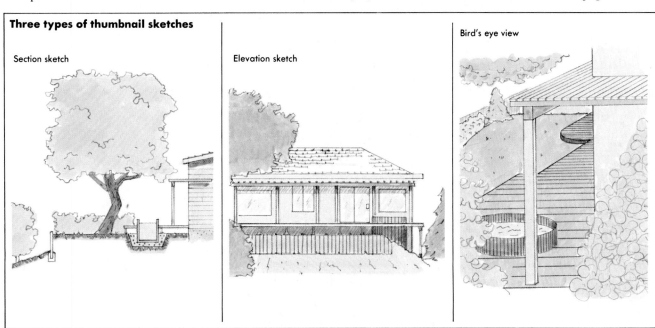

Three types of thumbnail sketches

Section sketch

Elevation sketch

Bird's eye view

WORKING DRAWINGS
PLANTING PLANS AND DETAILS

A working drawing is the final step in the planning and design process. From these drawings, you, or someone you hire, should have all the information necessary to install the landscape. The in-formation should be as exact and detailed as possible. Measure-ments, names and spac-ing of plants, the type of lumber for fences and decks, and any other information should be included. If the working drawing is done on tracing paper, it's easy to have sev-eral blueprints made. See text for details.

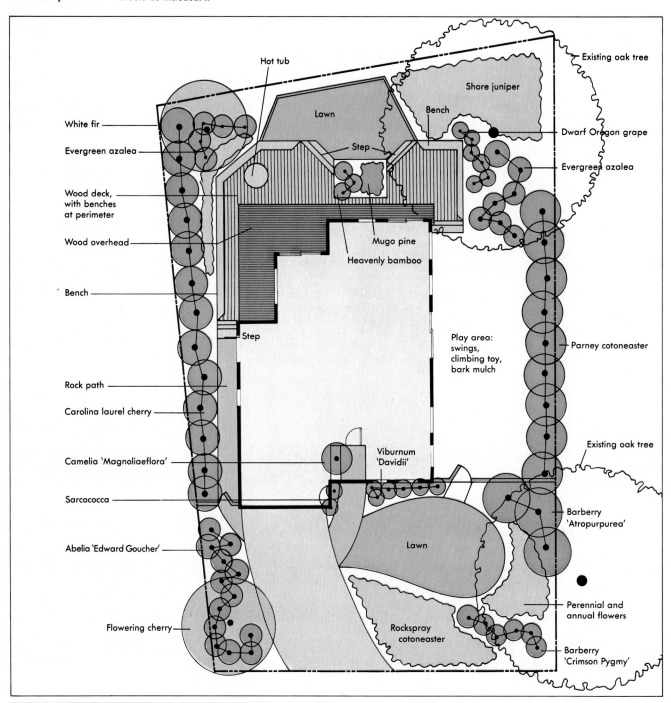

A working drawing is an accurate, scaled rendition of your final concept drawing. How much detail it has depends on how much information you need to remember or communicate to someone else (such as a contractor or city building inspector). Working drawings are so named because the information on them alone should enable you to do the work necessary for your landscape. A working drawing indicates graphically what kind, what size, and how many of each item you will need to complete the project. It also shows how to put the materials together to make the landscape.

Once you have combined the three or four best ideas into your final concept plan, check its elevations with simple sketches from different angles, and work through it again with a fresh overlay. Take the plan outside and walk around the spaces shown on paper. Use your imagination to test out the proposed design. How does it feel? Check to be sure that it includes everything you meant it to; access and circulation routes should be workable, and screening or view requirements should correspond to the notes you made earlier.

As you reevaluate, ask yourself, "Considering my time and budget, does this plan fill my needs?" Once you are sure that it does, trace the plant neatly, and use that tracing as the final plan.

Add measurements to all the spaces on the working drawing. Be exact and, wherever possible, use the standard sizes of available materials. For example, if you know that fencing material comes in 4-, 6-, and 8-foot lengths, don't decide to make a 6½-foot fence; it will create extra work and expense, and waste material. Although this may mean using dimensions that are slightly different from what was on your concept plan, it's better to make the changes at this stage than at the installation stage.

When it comes to thinking of problems you might encounter during construction, try to *overdo* it. Make *details*—these can be small sketches, elevations, sections, or other notations that show how you intend to solve potential problems. Sample details might include: How to dig a hole for a particular tree, how deep it should be, and what it will be backfilled with; how you intend to stake a group of new trees in a windy location; or specific ideas for the construction of a retaining wall.

On your working drawings, make notes of any detailed information you want to remember, such as the color of paint or stain for a fence, plant names and sizes, or water requirements for a special tree. Much of this information can be included in a *plant schedule*, either directly on the plan or on a second sheet.

When actually drawing the working plan, be sure to apply even pressure to your pencil to make a solid black line. Keep your lead sharp and remember to twirl the pencil as you draw, to ensure that the lines are even in width. Make the lines that represent important, solid features bolder and darker than lines for less significant items. For instance, steps and elevation differences should appear more bold than, say, handrailings. Indicate the eventual spread of trees by drawing circles with appropriate radii for each major plant, but also show what you intend to plant under the canopy of leaves. Remember to plant masses of the same type of plant for the greatest effect. Connect plants of the same type with light lines ending in an underlined notation of the plant name.

If you draw the plan on tracing paper, you can have an ozalid or a blueprint made of it. Both methods reproduce the drawing easily and inexpensively. Look in the yellow pages of your telephone book under "Blueprinters" for this service, and be sure to have five or six copies made at the same time; it usually costs no more than for one or two.

Landscape architect Lin Cotton works at a drawing table surrounded by natural light and a view of the landscape he designed for the pleasure it gives him.

ESTIMATING COSTS

To get an idea of the cost of improving your landscape, find out what and how many of each item you need. Make a rough estimate, based on the per-square-foot costs of the various materials you will need, before you have even finished your concept drawings. This will enable you to modify the plan, should you find that your estimate is dramatically over your budget, before you go to the trouble of making a working drawing.

To make a really accurate cost estimate, however, you must have a complete working drawing that spells out what and how many of each specific item is needed. We cannot give you exact prices, here, because of the regional differences in prices and the rapidly rising rates of most commodities; instead, we recommend that you check with your local suppliers before figuring a final cost estimate. But to give you some sense of comparative values, we have included many of the goods and services you will need to use, as well as their basic unit costs. Use this chart to weigh the relative costs of different treatments as you work your way through to the working drawings.

In making your cost estimate, list all the materials you will need from each different supplier. Put all the plant materials on one list, all the lumber on another, all the plumbing on yet another, and so on. Once this list is complete—that is, once it specifies the materials, the quantity required, the sizes and dimensions, the catalog numbers, and any other information that will help you order—call up the suppliers to find out who offers the best deal. Remember that quantity buying often brings prices down, and that the closer you are to the original source of the supplies, the lower the price should be.

Materials Cost Estimate (partial)

Phase One: Site Preparation

Drop box rental: three days use of 20 cubic yard box	$ 67.
Herbicide cost: for weed control	25.
Soil amendment: nitrified sawdust. 2" depth × 3500 square feet =21 cubic yards at $18.50 delivered (plus tax).	400.
Tiller rental: 1 day at $65. per day	65.
Tractor rental: ½ day at $50. per half day	50.
Phase One Subtotal	**$607.**

Phase Two: Drainage

Trencher rental: 5 hours at $15. per hour	$ 75.
Drain rock: 350 linear feet trench, at 1 cubic foot rock per 2 linear feet trench=170 cubic feet=6.5 cubic yards plus 15 cubic feet for 2 French drains=total of 7 cubic yards at $20. per yard delivered (plus tax)	155.
Drain line: 280'–3" perforated flex drain plus 100'–3" solid flex drain=total of 380' at 35 cents per foot	133.
Drain line fittings: 4- downspout connectors at $.60, 8- couplings at $.65, 6- "Y" connectors at $1.60, 3- tee connectors at $1.20, and 7- end caps at $.80 (plus tax)	28.
Phase Two Subtotal	**$391.**

Phase Three: Construction

Concrete walks: forms – 300' 1×4 at $.25=$75. 200' bender board at $.16=$32. concrete: 150' path length=3.5' width=4" depth =175 cubic feet finished concrete. This equals 7 cubic yards bulk ready mix at $22. per yard delivered (plus tax)=$154. reinforcing mesh: 525 square feet at $.30 per square foot plus tax=$170. Total for concrete paths	$585.
Exposed aggregate concrete patio: forms - 400'- 2×4" rough redwood forms (permanent headers) at $.40 per foot	160.
Phase Three Subtotal	**$745.**

Plant list

Trees

Number	Size	Botanical name	Common name	Notes
1	15 gal	Prunus yedoensis 'Akebono'	Flowering cherry	
1	15 gal	Abies concolor	White Fir	When large enough, prune so that the lowest branch is 7' from the ground

Shrubs

Number	Size	Botanical name	Common name	Notes
9	5 gal	Cotoneaster lacteus	Parney cotoneaster	Prune to an informal hedge
1	5 gal	Pinus mugo 'mugo'	Mugo pine	
1	5 gal	Camelia japonica 'Magnoliaeflora'	Camelia	
13	1 gal	Prunus caroliniana	Carolina laurel cherry	Prune to an informal hedge

LEGAL CONSIDERATIONS

Building permits and city ordinances

Getting city hall to approve your construction plans can be an important part of making a landscape. If you plan to make improvements over your property line onto city land, or if you are building a structure that falls under the review of the building department, your working drawings will need to be checked by the proper authority.

Planting, irrigating, paving, and other simple improvements usually are exempt from city review; however, fences, almost all building structures, electrical work, and most plumbing work require a building permit and, in many cities, physical inspection of the work.

If you have any any question about whether or not you need a permit or other approval, play it safe and check with your local building department. Remember, the building department is there to serve you and to keep you from making costly and possibly dangerous mistakes. Avoiding the inspection process may save you a small fee and a bit of inconvenience, but it also may end up causing you a lot of trouble if you have not followed the code.

Most local planning agencies have zoning regulations that require setbacks, or borders to lot lines. In some areas, zoning often limits the percentage of the lot that can be covered with buildings or paving. Some localities even have tree ordinances to protect so-called "Heritage Trees" that are considered the rightful property of the entire community, even though they happen to be growing on private property. Be sure to thoroughly check out any regulations that might apply to the work you plan to do.

If it turns out that the improvements you want to make indeed will conflict with established zoning regulations, you can often ask for a variance. A variance is an exception to the regulations, and is given by the local appeal board when there are reasonable arguments in favor of an exception.

Variances are intended to provide a bit of flexibility to the hard-and-fast safety and quality standards of urban development. If your proposal is reasonable and doesn't interfere with a neighbor's interests, the local planning board will probably give you the go-ahead.

However, in order to apply for approval, you have to submit at least two prints of your plans that show your intentions clearly. Working drawings are an excellent way to indicate your plans. If you think you will need a variance, check with your local building department for the established procedure.

Contractors and contracts

If you decide to hire a contractor to install your landscape, most of them will require you to sign a contract before they begin actual work. Be sure to read the entire contract and to add any paragraphs necessary to protect your interest. Also be sure that the contract requires the contractor to follow your plans and specifications. To ensure that you aren't left with a half-finished job, it's wise to require, in writing, that the work be finished by a certain date. You can do this by establishing a per-day penalty clause in the contract; this will give the contractor an incentive to work steadily through to completion on your project.

Most contracts require an initial deposit or advance. This is reasonable, since the contractor will be ordering materials that he may have to pay for in advance. But make sure to indicate in the contract that a portion of the total fee is payable 2 to 4 weeks after the scheduled completion date. This stipulation means, in effect, that any final details will be attended to relatively quickly.

Many states have strict legislation governing home improvements done by contractors. Most of these laws protect the consumer. Familiarize yourself with these laws before starting any projects.

Whenever you hire people to work on your property, remember that there may be lien liabilities if the contractor—or you—fail to pay them. If a contractor hires subcontractors to carry out some of the work and then fails to pay them, they can make a claim against you, the property owner. For instance, a contractor hired to do some work may subcontract out a portion of it, accept your initial deposit, and then go out of business. If he didn't pay the subcontractor for the work performed, you may find yourself subject to a lien against your property, which you'll have to pay off before the property is refinanced or sold. Since it's best to avoid liens at all costs, pay the contractor in increments; that way you will always have enough money in reserve to pay for the subcontracted work if the contractor does not.

CRITICAL PATH

As you set out to construct your landscape, you may find that a critical path will help you with your planning. This is a graphic representation of the order in which you have to do things to get the job done.

To make a critical path, work back through the tasks described in Chapter Six, noting the ones that apply to you. Estimate how long each one will take, and then double that estimate—it always takes longer to do things than you think it will.

Using a fresh piece of paper, draw a horizontal line to represent the direct progress of the project. Then put the tasks in the sequence that will create a smooth progression. Figure in such things as renting equipment and hiring extra help for those phases of the work that seem more than you can handle alone. In dealing with concrete, allow yourself enough time to finish the preparations completely before the delivery truck arrives; also, be sure to have all the extra help you need to work the material while it is still pliable.

Just because you've ordered your materials already doesn't mean that there are no more decisions to make. In fact, when you pick up your materials, be ready to make even more decisions. In general, be on the lookout for any flaws in quality. Check plant material for form, root-bound problems, and general vigor. Make sure that any lumber you buy is free of flaws. Check the quantities of all materials to make sure you aren't getting fewer than you ordered.

If you plan to put working drawings out for bids by contractors, make sure that the job description includes everything you want done. Specify the quality of each material required; if you don't, a contractor (wishing to submit the winning bid) may use the least expensive material suitable for the job. To prevent such an occurrence, spell out your exact expectations on the plans themselves, or write up separate specifications. Your plans and specifications will become part of your contract documents, and they will assure both you and the contractor of exactly what is to be done.

INSTALLING YOUR LANDSCAPE

If you've done a good job with the design tools at hand, installing your landscape should be a straightforward task. If you decide to do the job yourself, you'll do your fair share of hard work, but watching your design come to life makes all the effort worthwhile.

For gentle curves and bold lines in the landscape, use bender board. These flexible wood strips can be made into headers, as they are here, or used as concrete forms to make paths, patios, or mowing strips.

The sweep of this path and the balance of the landscape are the products of careful and sensitive planning. But they also required tools and techniques to make the design an actuality.

Now that you have designed your landscape, at last it is time to take your shovel in hand and begin moving soil. But first explain to the people you live with that the yard may be a shambles for a time. However, you can shorten that time by thinking out your schedule carefully; this will spare your family (and you) from having to stare for weeks at piles of soil sitting in the yard, waiting to be spread.

We have broken the installation process into 12 steps (see page 72). There are natural pauses between steps—points at which you can clean up, wipe your brow, and bask in the glow of a job well done. If your timetable forces you to take breaks, these pauses are good places to take them; you won't be leaving piles of materials, open ditches, or unfinished construction that is liable to be damaged.

Different steps take varying lengths of time. Here's a good rule of thumb: Estimate your time for a job very carefully, then double that estimate—a job always takes longer than you anticipate (even for professional contractors).

You may not be able to really see the results of some of these steps—for instance, the yard will look just about the same after you've installed the sprinkler system and wiring for the outside lights as it did before you began. If you begin to feel that you haven't accomplished very much, considering the hundreds of dollars and days of time you've spent, take heart—some of these steps are *supposed* to be invisible. A sprinkler system or drain line is meant to be out of sight, so that it can maintain the more visible part of a beautiful garden.

On the other hand, some aspects of the job seem to go very quickly. This is why construction is very satisfying—as soon as you have finished all or part of a construction project, you can look at your new deck or gazebo and feel proud, capable, and visually dazzled. Planting contains the seeds of the same magic; you are apt to feel an intense satisfaction when you look at a finished landscape with all its plants in place and its newly sodded lawn.

But not all the steps give this kind of emotional feedback. Especially at the beginning of the project, be prepared to catch yourself worrying that the work is going too slowly, that you are not getting enough done. When you do catch these worries, take comfort in the thought that you are laying the foundation of your garden, and that whatever time and money you are spending here will prevent headaches and make your life easier for many years to come.

If you do each step carefully, paying attention to the small details, and if you buy the best quality you can afford, your garden will grow and ripen. Year by year, it will give you more satisfaction, and it won't fall prey to the many small ills that make gardening a chore instead of the immensely satisfying occupation it should be.

THE 12 STEPS

The 12 steps to installing a landscape

Not all of these steps will be necessary for each job, nor must they always be done in this order. For instance, you may find it more convenient to install the sprinkler system (step 6) before you install headers (step 5).

1 Clear the site down to bare soil; leave only those plants and features that will be included in the new landscape.

2 Rough grade, making major contour changes.

3 Install a drain system.

4 Do masonry and wood construction.

5 Install headers.

6 Install sprinkler system and any other underground lines, such as gas or electric lines.

7 Spread fertilizers and soil amendments. Cultivate.

8 Level to the final grade.

9 Plant 1-gallon and larger plants.

10 Plant bedding plants, ground covers, and lawns.

11 Clean up.

12 Aftercare until plants are established.

Renting tools

These days, you can rent an amazing variety of hand and power tools from hardware stores or rental agencies. This list is representative; ask your local rental agency for a price list showing the tools they have available.

The type of tools available from rental agencies

Axe	Backpack Blower	Seed Spreader	Sod Cutter
Hole Spoon	Gas Chain Saw	Scythe	Aerator
Hand Leveler	Electric Chain Saw	Hand Dirt Tamper	Rototiller
Mattock	Limb Chipper	Rebar Cutter	Trencher
Front End Loader with Scraper	Electric Hedge Trimmer	String Weed Trimmer	Horizontal Boring Machine
Steel Post Driver	Lawn Edger	Wheelbarrow	Yard Vacuum
Post Hole Digger	Lawn Mower	Crowbar	Electric Dirt Spade
Pole Pruner	Weed Mower	Builder's Level	Pick
Pole Saw	Flail Mower	Cement Finishing Tools	Cement Mixer
Wide Rake	Lawn Roller	Railroad Tie Saw	Concrete Saw
Electric Jack Hammer	Power Post Hole Digger	Dirt Rammer	Cement Vibrator
Fertilizer Spreader	Lawn Renovator	Rebar Bender	

STEP 1: CLEAN THE SITE

When putting in your landscape, the first step is to clear the place where you plan to work. There are three categories of material to be cleaned away: debris, weeds, and construction features.

Picking up debris

Picking up debris is a less-than-inspirational task, one that you might consider hiring someone else to do. Often, a local high school or college student will be available to help you. But don't just give a friendly wave and go indoors to read—work *with* your assistant. Otherwise you may find that the job wasn't done according to your plan.

You can also rent a debris box from most garbage-collection departments. This time-saving device saves you the trouble of loading a truck and hauling its contents to the dump (which could constitute a good half of the cleanup job). Make sure to place the box as close to the site you are cleaning as possible.

Weed control

Weeds can create two troublesome situations, but forethought and planning will save you a great deal of anguish later on. The first problem involves difficult perennial weeds such as Bermudagrass, couchgrass, or bindweed. If these weeds are cut off or tilled in, they will resprout full strength just about when you are ready to sit back and enjoy your brand-new landscape.

If the weeds are actively growing at the time you wish to remove them, spray them with Kleenup herbicide (glysophate), wait a week, and then remove them. They may not look dead yet, but the herbicide has indeed killed their roots. (By the way, Kleenup breaks down quickly in the soil, so it won't poison further plantings.)

However, if the weeds are not actively growing, you can take them out immediately if you wish, using a soil fumigant. But this is a serious step; fumigants kill everything in the soil, and are difficult to use properly. The best thing to do, if you can, is to *plan* your weed-control operation. If you remove existing weeds before they go to seed in the spring or summer, you will have far fewer seeds in the soil to deal with.

However, if you *do* have weed seeds left in the soil (and this constitutes the second problem), you will have to deal with them somehow. If your yard has been wild or weedy for some time, your soil probably is laced with weed seeds. You can ignore them temporarily—which is easy to do, since you can't see them—but later on you'll be spending your weekends pulling weeds instead of simply enjoying your garden.

Here's one simple way to remove weed seeds: Schedule a pause of two weeks to a month in your landscaping before you start planting. During this pause, keep the soil damp to encourage weed-seed germination. When you are ready to begin planting (but before any of the new weeds go to seed), spray them with a contact herbicide that leaves no soil residue. If you hoe the weeds or till them in, you will stir up the soil, bringing new weed seeds to the surface to germinate.

Removing trees and shrubs

If cut off at soil level, some vigorous trees and shrubs will sprout from the roots. You can prevent resprouting by killing the plant with a brushkiller-type herbicide before it threatens to sprout. Either spray it on the foliage, or make downward-slanting cuts into the bark and pour brushkiller into those cuts. Whichever method you choose, follow the directions on the label.

If you can keep from having to remove stumps, by all means do so; stump grubbing is probably the hardest, slowest work you will encounter in your landscape project. If the area does not need to be cultivated, you can cut the stump off just below ground level and leave it. Over the years it will rot, leaving a depression that will need to be filled in.

If you must remove the stump, and if it's a large one, consider hiring a tree service. They will bring in stump grinders, large machines that will reduce a stump to chips in just minutes.

Removing lawns

If you want to clear an area of grass but could use the turf in another place, by all means save it. Rent a sodcutter, or use a sharp spade to cut the turf from the ground, taking ¾ inch of soil with it. Cut the sod into strips of one width (12 to 18 inches is convenient), and lay them out on a flat surface in a shady location (a patio or driveway works well). If watered carefully, sod will stay healthy for weeks.

However, even if you don't need the sod, or if it is in too poor a condition to use, you still have to remove it. If your particular grass becomes dormant (turns brown) in the winter, first kill it with an herbicide containing glysophate. The deep root-systems of these grasses will resprout even after you have removed the sod.

Once you have removed the sod, you can put it to use—it makes compost. Just stack it upside down, sprinkling a little fertilizer or manure between the layers. After it has rotted, use the compost in the vegetable garden or annual bed.

Above: A rented debris box cuts the work of cleaning the landscape site.
Right: If you are removing Bermudagrass or other deep-rooted lawn grasses, kill them first with an herbicide to keep the grass from becoming a troublesome weed later.
Below: After the grass is dead, remove the sod with a sod cutter.

STEP 2: ROUGH GRADE

Now it is time to do most of the soil moving. Try to plan your project so that you won't have to either buy or dump any soil —both actions are expensive. If you can, shape your yard by moving soil around; if you need to build up a low spot, try to find a high spot to take the needed soil from.

Buying soil

If you must buy soil, match the texture of your existing soil. It's not necessary to buy the same soil, with all its present problems. If you have a heavy clay soil that drains slowly, buy a *good* clay soil that drains well. But resist the temptation to lighten it with a sandy loam. Soils of radically different textures can cause drainage problems if they aren't mixed perfectly; water does not move easily from one soil texture to the other.

Soil is sold by the cubic yard. The minimum load most contractors will deliver without a surcharge is 5 yards. Quality varies from soil to soil, as with most products you might buy. Some dealers may sell soil for three times as much as others. You probably do not need to buy the highest quality available, but steer clear of the lowest quality—it will be troublesome later on. Price a number of different suppliers, then investigate those that interest you. Find out where their stockpile is, and drive out to see the soil before you order. It's hard to refuse a delivery from a dump truck that's backed into your yard.

One other hint: Have the soil dumped as close to where it will be spread as possible, even if this means taking out a section of fence or filling in a ditch to gain access to the back yard. A good dump-truck driver can spread the load to the depth you ask with remarkable precision, saving you much work later.

Moving soil

If you use only a shovel and wheelbarrow to move soil, the work will be difficult and laborious. Instead, why not use hired labor, or rent a tractor? Rental agencies carry a wide assortment of tractors in homeowner sizes. These make the job faster and easier, and they are fun to work, too. You may even find that you are sorry when the job is over and you have to return the tractor. Rent the largest size you can maneuver in your yard. But first measure its width carefully to make sure you can get it *into* the yard.

Measuring soil level

In most cases, you will be able to make your grade change by eye, without more formal measuring. However, if you need to make a critical or extensive grade change, there are two devices that can help you.

For short distances, buy a *line level*, a small spirit level with a pair of hooks that suspend it from a horizontal line. Attach a piece of mason's line to the tops of two stakes (drive the stakes into the ground firmly enough that you can pull all the slack from the line), and hang the level at one end of the line. It will tell you whether the line is level or when the stakes are at the same height.

For more complex jobs or long distances, rent a *builder's level* from your rental agency. This instrument looks like a surveyor's transit, but it is much simpler to use.

Set the level on its tripod in the center of the yard; ideally, you want to be able to see from this location all the points you wish to measure. Now level the tripod and

This rented tractor not only speeds up the heavy work of moving soil, but can actually make the job fun. Tractors are available in a range of sizes, from this back yard model made for working in tight quarters, to full-size construction tractors. They also come with a variety of blade, bucket and scraper attachments.

look through the telescope. You will see a horizontal line on the lens that crosses the point that is level with the instrument.

Levels are used with a surveyor's rod or a tape measure. Have an assistant stand the rod on a reference point (the corner of a patio or sidewalk works well). Record the number intersected by the line when you sight on the rod through the level. Take similar sightings on any point in the landscape you wish to measure. The distance above or below the reference number is the height above or below your reference point. Remember, a lower number means that the ground is *higher*. Mark the measured points with surveyor's stakes (buy them from a lumber yard) with the elevation written on them.

Wherever you plan to add soil, first drive in stakes; their tops should be at the level you want to fill up with soil. These will serve as guides for the leveling process.

Before you remove any large amounts of soil, strip off the topsoil (usually the top 6 to 12 inches) and pile it to one side to redistribute later on. This soil is valuable for plant growth, so don't bury it.

This builder's level helps you to find the precise elevation of any point in your yard. Use it in the planning stages to determine the amount of fill you need or to measure a slope. Use it again when you install your landscape to help level soil, make cuts, fill in low spots, or pitch a drain line just right.

Judging soil quality

The best garden soil is soft, friable, and free of rocks and weed seeds; it also drains well.

A handful of good soil is dark-colored and like cake crumbs. Its softness and darkness are due to its high humus content. A moist clod breaks easily into crumbs and is not sticky. There are few rocks; those present are pebbles. There is no trash, such as sticks or building material, in the soil.

If you have time, you can test for the presence of weed seeds by germinating a sample of the soil. Spread the soil an inch deep in a nursery flat or on a cookie sheet. Keep the soil moist and warm (70-80° F.) for two weeks. Any weed seeds present in the soil will have germinated by this time.

The best way to judge how well a soil drains is to dig a hole and fill it with water. After the water drains out, fill it again and measure how fast the water level drops. Less than 1 inch per hour means that it drains slowly and will give you trouble. If you can't make this test in the yard itself, take a sample of soil home and test it in a tin can, as illustrated.

Testing Drainage

Water

Soil

Holes punched in bottom of can covered with window screen or cheesecloth

Drop the can on a hard surface a few times to settle the soil. Measure drainage only after water is dripping freely from the bottom of can.

How to judge soil texture:

If the soil is dry:	■ Sandy soil forms a weak clod that shatters into powder when squeezed. ■ Loamy soil forms a moderately strong clod that breaks, but does not shatter, in your hand. ■ Clay soil forms a hard clod that cannot be broken with bare hands.
If the soil is moist:	■ Sandy soil is gritty between the fingers; clods break at a touch. ■ Loamy soil is soft between the fingers; clods break easily into soft crumbs. ■ Clay soil is very sticky; clods are plastic—they do not break, but deform.

STEP 3: DRAINAGE

The most important drainage provision you can make is *surface drainage*. If it is at all possible, slope the ground so that water will be carried away from your property. Ideally, you would have 2 or 3 feet of fall for every 100 feet of horizontal land. The slightness of this slope moves water to a storm sewer or drainage ditch without letting it stand or puddle, but moves it slowly enough that no erosion problems result.

Be particularly careful not to shape the ground so that it will carry water to the house. The land should slope away from your house for at least 2 feet on all sides. In addition, make sure that your yard does not discharge its water onto your neighbor's property.

Drain lines

Drain lines are pipes that are laid in a ditch and buried. Holes cut in the lower side of the pipes allow excess water to enter them and then be carried away. Drain lines are valuable for lowering a water table. If a hole dug in your yard slowly fills with water, that means your water table is too high. A drain line will lower the water table to the level of the line. Often, it will help a soil to drain more quickly after rain.

However, if the reason that your soil drains slowly is because it is a heavy clay, a drain line won't help you—it's the nature of heavy clay soil to drain water slowly. Instead, slope your soil properly and improve its structure so that water can enter it more easily (see Step 6).

Catch basins

A catch basin is a vertical pipe in the ground into which water can run. A pipe system resembling that of a drain line leads the water from the catch basin to a drainage ditch or storm sewer.

You can buy catch basins ready-made or you can make your own from concrete or redwood. They are usually covered with a grate, but you can fill them with rocks, instead. Catch basins are useful in low spots where surface drainage will not work, or where there is a particularly heavy flow of water.

Modern drain lines are lightweight, flexible, and simple to install. Use this type of line to lower a high water table, carry water away from low spots, and collect the runoff from a slope or the house downspouts.

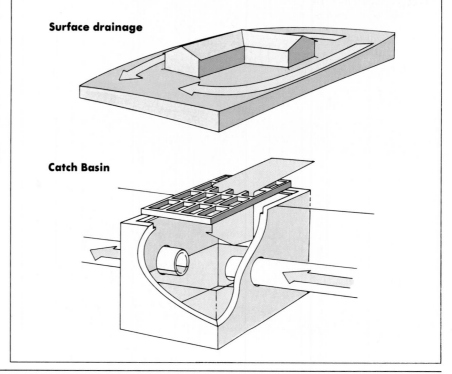

Surface drainage

Catch Basin

Installing a drain line

To plan a drain line, first determine where the water will go once it leaves the line. Usually it will go into a storm sewer, gutter, or drainage ditch. The point at which the water leaves the drain line is called the *outfall*. The elevation of the outfall determines the construction of the rest of the system. Since water moves through the line by gravity, there must be a fall from the top end to the bottom end of the line. In addition, there must be enough downward slope so that the speed of the water will keep silt in suspension. There must be at least a 1-foot drop for every 100 feet of line, or else eventually the drain line will fill up with silt and stop functioning.

To find out how deep you can place the line, start with the elevation of the outfall and measure backwards. The deeper the line, the deeper the water table will be.

Plan to use a herringbone pattern, keeping the lines from 10 to 20 feet apart. If you have only one low area in your yard, you probably won't need to put more than a single line under it.

Start digging the ditch at the outfall, and work back into your yard. Try to maintain a steady slope (minimum of a 1-foot rise per 100 feet of ditch, or ⅛ inch per foot) without dips, no matter what the shape of the soil is. A simple level that can help you is described in the illustration. As you dig the ditch, drag this level behind you to measure an even 1 percent.

If the bottom of the ditch is rocky or broken, cover it with a 1-inch layer of sand or fine soil to make an even bed for the drain line.

Modern drain lines usually are made of a flexible, corrugated plastic hose. This hose will make all but the sharpest bends without joining, and it is light and simple to install. You can buy it in 3- and 4-inch diameters. The 4-inch hose offers the advantage of being less likely to clog if a piece of debris or a small animal gets stuck in it.

Always lay the drain lines with the holes *down*. This prevents soil from dropping into the line. It also lowers the water table to the bottom of the line rather than to the level of the top. (Water rises into the line.)

An effective drain system must be surrounded by an envelope of rock. This will protect the line, keep soil from entering it, and increase the capacity of the line by conducting water itself. You can use either smooth river-rock or crushed rock—the former drains faster, but the latter gives greater mechanical strength. Whichever you use, backfill the ditch with the drain rock to a depth of 4 inches over the line. Then install a "clean-out"—an access hole

—at the highest point of the system.

Now take the soil that you removed from the ditch and shovel it back in again, backfilling the ditch to ground level. But before the ditch is *quite* full, run water into it to settle the soil; this will keep it from settling later on, after you've planted a lawn over it. You can also use this method to ensure that any ditches dug for sprinkler systems or electric lines will settle.

A variation on the drain line involves filling the ditch with drain rock up to the surface. This allows surface water to enter the line quickly, and catches the water that runs off a slope before it gets to your garden.

To keep soil out of the rock on the surface, place a couple of 2 x 6 headers on either side of the ditch, making sure that they extend an inch or two above ground level. The result of this will be a gravel path that drains very quickly.

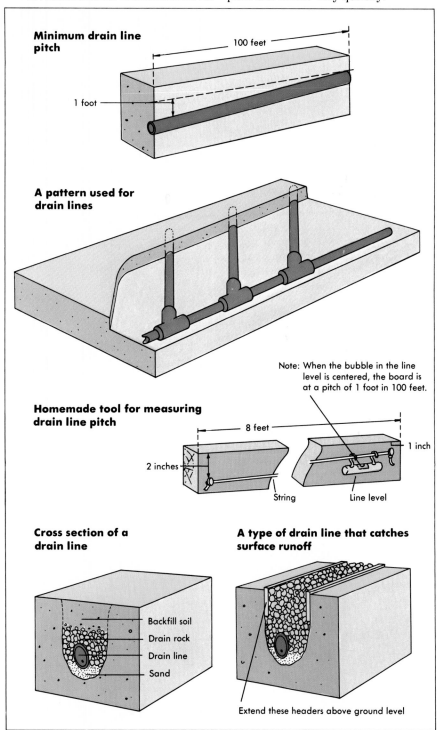

Minimum drain line pitch

100 feet

1 foot

A pattern used for drain lines

Note: When the bubble in the line level is centered, the board is at a pitch of 1 foot in 100 feet.

Homemade tool for measuring drain line pitch

8 feet

2 inches

1 inch

String

Line level

Cross section of a drain line

Backfill soil

Drain rock

Drain line

Sand

A type of drain line that catches surface runoff

Extend these headers above ground level

STEP 4: CONSTRUCTION

By now, your yard is shaped just the way you want it, and you know that it won't puddle up in a rain. You have stretched and sized the canvas upon which you will paint your landscape. The construction you do in this step will amount to the first rough lines drawn on your blank canvas.

As the heavy lumber trucks or cement mixers make their deliveries into your yard, remember that there's a drain line under the surface. This line will withstand some pressure, but not as much as a full cement mixer will exert. So direct traffic attentively.

The subject of garden construction is a vast one. For detailed instructions on a wide variety of garden projects, see Ortho's book, *Garden Construction Know-how*. In this book, however, we will mention just two aspects.

Retaining walls

You can build low retaining walls (under 3 feet) yourself, using a variety of methods; but since retaining walls over 3 feet must hold back a great deal of weight, you probably would do best to leave them to a contractor.

Remember that soil has a tendency to flow downhill; therefore it will press against the back of the retaining wall. Since it is the water in the soil that causes it to flow, you must make sure that water can drain out of the soil you are retaining. To do this, you can either make "weep holes" every few feet near the bottom of the wall, or you can lay down drain tile horizontally behind the wall so that the tile will catch and carry away water.

Dry-laid rock: Rock or broken sidewalk pieces laid against a bank will keep the face of the bank from eroding. This method works well for a low wall. Slope the bank a minimum of 2 inches for each foot of height, and lay the stones that face it at an angle into the bank, so that the bank supports their weight. Rock retaining walls are appealing in a natural or informal landscape. Plant succulents or rock plants in the crevices to soften the effect still more.

Vertical wood members: Sections of treated log or railroad ties adapt well to curves in a landscape. Be sure to anchor them deeply in the ground to keep them from leaning out. A good rule of thumb is: Put as much wood below the ground as there is above. For added strength, set the wood members in a trench and pour concrete around them. Connect them on the upper back side with a continuous strip of 8-inch-wide sheet metal.

Wood walls: Wood, the most common material for retaining walls, makes a neat wall that lends itself to both formal and informal designs. If you build the wall 16 to 18 inches high, you can put a cap on top to double as a garden seat.

Left: This retaining wall of vertical railroad ties lends strength to a dry "pond." Below: Cobbles make a delightful and easy retaining wall. They are still available in many cities; look for them where streets are being reconstructed.

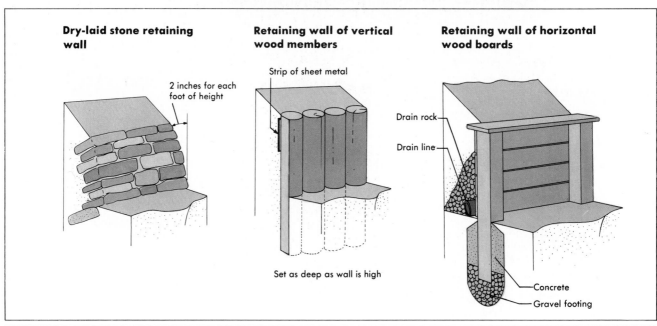

Dry-laid stone retaining wall

2 inches for each foot of height

Retaining wall of vertical wood members

Strip of sheet metal

Set as deep as wall is high

Retaining wall of horizontal wood boards

Drain rock

Drain line

Concrete

Gravel footing

Left: This walk of flag-
stones set in concrete
is permanent and trou-
ble-free.
Below: Decomposed
granite paths offer
many of the benefits
of masonry paths with-
out the cost and effort
of installation. Build
the path in 1-inch lay-
ers, wetting and roll-
ing each layer.

Walks

The simplest walk to install is one made
of stepping stones. You can use a wide
variety of materials, ranging from masonry steps to log rounds or railroad ties.

At the opposite extreme is a solid
walk of poured concrete, brick, or stone
set in mortar. To make this type of walk,
see Ortho's book, *Garden Construction
Know-How.*

A third method of constructing paths
is to use a loose aggregate. You can use
gravel and bark or wood chips, but like
most loose materials they shift under your
feet and make walking difficult.

In most areas, you can buy soft rock
aggregate such as decomposed granite,
shale, or bluestone. In hardness, these materials are about midway between gravel
and soil. They pack into a firm surface like
soil, but they don't become muddy or support weed growth.

Use strong headers on each side of
the path, and cross headers as steps or for
decoration. Excavate 2 to 4 inches deep,
then spread the aggregate in 1-inch-deep
layers, wetting and rolling or tamping it
firmly between layers. Crown the surface
slightly so that it will shed water. This
path will become harder with use. To
maintain it, level it occasionally with the
back of a rake.

STEP 5:
INSTALL HEADERS

Headers are wood or masonry edges around lawns or planting beds. They give a crisp, professional look to a garden and make maintenance easier.

Masonry headers

Brick makes attractive and permanent headers. Or you can pour concrete between bender board forms to make curves. Pour wide (6 inches wider than the header) concrete pads under either brick or concrete headers. (See Ortho's book *Garden Construction Know-How* for details on concrete and brick work.)

Wood Headers

Use only the heartwood of redwood, cedar, or cypress. Other woods will rot in a few years.

For the greatest strength, make headers of 2 x 4 material nailed to 2 x 3 stakes a foot or more long. Dig a trench, lay the headers in it, and stake them in place every 4 to 6 feet. Place the stakes on alternate sides of the header. Drive them in until the stake is almost flush with the header and nail it in place with two 8 penny galvanized nails. Saw off the top of the stake at a 45-degree angle.

Bender Board

Bender board, available in lumber yards, is made of strips of wood about ³/₈ inch thick and 4 inches wide. It is used to make curved concrete forms as well as curved headers.

If you want it to last in the ground for years, choose bender board that's made of heartwood, not sapwood. Sapwood (even

of redwood or cedar) rots quickly in soil. The bender board should be uniform in thickness and flexible enough to form tight curves without breaking.

To install it, dig a trench and pound in 1 x 2 stakes to hold the bender board in place temporarily. Wet the bender board for greater flexibility. Once you have put it just where you want it, drive in more stakes, as needed. There should be a stake every 3 feet (closer on curves), at every joint, and on either side of the board at the ends. Drive the tops of the stakes an inch or so below the top of the board.

Put in enough nails to hold the board in place, then place another board behind it, and, for maximum strength, a third board. Stagger the joints and place new stakes at each joint. Nail all boards to the stakes with 8 penny galvanized nails.

Top-nail the bender boards together every 6 inches between stakes to keep them from spreading with age. With a sledge hammer head behind the boards, drive a nail through all three boards at a 45-degree angle. When the nail hits the hammer head, it will turn and clinch itself into the wood.

After the bender boards are in place, drive stakes every 3 feet, at all the joints, and on both sides of the bender board at the ends. Hold a hammer head behind the board to drive the nails more easily.

Laying out curves

Here are three methods for laying out a curve in your landscape:

1. *Draw a line with a stick.* This method works well for ground that is soft and even-textured. If you work around the line, however, it scuffs away easily.

2. *Draw a line with lime.* Holding a bucket of agricultural lime in your left hand, dribble the lime with your right hand. This line is almost scuff-proof, but if you don't get it right the first time, you can correct it with a rake. This is a good way to try out proportions of things in the planning stages; you can draw your whole landscape on the ground.

3. *Lay down a hose.* A garden hose makes an excellent line to experiment with. Push it this way and that until it looks just right.

STEP 6: INSTALL IRRIGATION

If you live in an area where you have to water your yard more than a few times a year, a permanent irrigation system can save you an enormous amount of time and work. You have three watering options: You can place faucets at convenient locations and water with garden hoses; you can install a permanent underground sprinkler system; or you can install a drip irrigation system.

Garden hoses

This is by far the least expensive option, requiring perhaps only a couple of hoses and some sprinkler heads. But, depending on your location, you may spend hours a week moving sprinklers from one spot to another.

Sprinkler system

This type of system can cost hundreds or thousands of dollars to install, but over the years it will save you many hundreds or thousands of hours of hand watering. Automatic sprinkler systems usually take better care of your plants, too—the clock never lets the garden go "just one more day" before watering, and never floods it by forgetting to turn the sprinklers off.

Drip irrigation system

This type of permanent irrigation system is radically different from a sprinkler system. It consists of tubes and hoses that carry water to every plant in the yard (except for lawns and ground covers). The system is on for hours each day, dripping water slowly into the soil. Since it operates under low pressure (5 to 25 pounds per square inch), the materials are inexpensive. But since the water must be carried to each plant, there is a lot of material to purchase. A complete system generally costs as much to install as a comparable sprinkler system. Up until recently, drip systems had major engineering difficulties; however, the technology has grown to the point where a properly designed drip system can be as trouble-free as a sprinkler system. Plants grow better when drip irrigated because their roots receive a constant supply of water without ever being starved or flooded. But, because the technology is new, you may have trouble finding someone to design or install one for you.

Above: A permanently installed sprinkler system is an investment that pays off in a beautiful garden. These rotating lawn heads water gently and evenly.
Below: Components of a drip irrigation system.

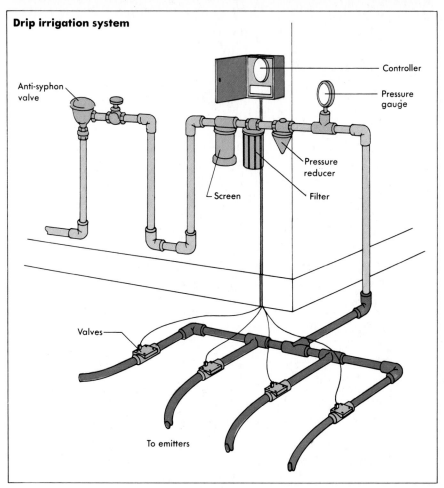

Drip irrigation system

Anti-syphon valve

Controller

Pressure gauge

Screen

Pressure reducer

Filter

Valves

To emitters

INSTALLING A SPRINKLER SYSTEM

Since a complete sprinkler system represents a significant investment, you may be tempted to cut corners, locate heads too far apart, and use smaller valves. But resist this temptation; don't compromise. If you can't afford a complete system now, do a good job on just part of your yard; put in the rest of the system later on, when you *can* afford it. Money well spent now will be trouble saved for years to come.

The following are general instructions, meant to give you an overview. For more specific details, follow the manufacturer's instructions for the particular components you select.

Collect information

Before you begin, there are a few pieces of information you will need to gather.

Find the flow rate: Buy a pressure gauge or borrow one from your sprinkler parts supplier. Attach it to an outside faucet and open the valve. What you are reading is the water pressure in pounds per square inch. Take the reading at the time of day when you expect to be using the sprinkler system the most—this pressure can vary according to the time of day or even the day of the week, depending on how many of your neighbors are using water.

You will also need to know the size of your water meter (usually it is ⅝ inch, ¾ inch, or 1 inch). Read this information from the meter itself, or ask the water department to tell you.

You should know the size of your service line (the line from the water meter to the house). Wrap a piece of string around the pipe on the house side of the water meter, and measure the length of the string. Then check *Chart 1* to find out the pipe size.

Using this information, find your flow rate from *Chart 2*. The flow rate, in gallons per minute, is the amount of water available to run your sprinkler system. You will need this information to specify sprinkler heads.

Catalogs: Get a catalog of sprinkler irrigation parts from an irrigation dealer. These catalogs contain specifications for sprinkler heads, valves, and the other parts you will need.

A sprinkler system is particularly helpful if you have a difficult irrigation problem, such as a steep slope or a complex planting plan.

Chart 1: Service line size

Length of string	2¾″	3¼″	3½″	4″	4⅜″	5″
Size of copper tubing service line	¾″	—	1″	—	1¼″	—
Size of galvanized pipe service line	—	¾″	—	1″	—	1¼″

Chart 2: Flow rate in gallons per minute (GPM)

Water meter size	Service line size	Water pressure *30	40	50	60	70	80PSI and above
⅝″	¾″	7	9	10	10	10	10
	1″	9	12	18	18	18	18
	1¼″	10	14	20	20	20	20
¾″	¾″	7	9	10	10	10	10
	1″	9	14	18	18	18	18
	1¼″	10	22	30	30	30	30
1″	¾″	7	10	10	10	10	10
	1″	9	18	18	18	18	18
	1¼″	12	30	30	30	30	30

*Based on a full flow (no corrosion or restrictions) pipe 75′ long
These two charts courtesy of Rain Bird Sprinkler Mfg. Corp.

Designing the system

Working with a base plan of your landscape, design each element of your sprinkler system as you read about it in this book. Work with tracing paper overlays so that you can try ideas and throw them away without having to erase. Each of the three steps illustrated here can be on a separate overlay; this way, your final plan won't be so cluttered.

It will be easier to show all the fittings and parts if you begin with a large-scale plan, as large as you can conveniently fit on your drawing board. Also, keep your notes on the plan as small as possible to save space.

Don't be in a hurry with the design. Try many ideas and ways of designing the system. The system will slowly evolve as you try different methods, until you know that you have an irrigation plan that will do just what you want it to.

When you measured your yard for a landscape design, accuracy was only important in showing relative proportions of various areas. If the lawn is actually a little larger and the flower bed a little smaller than the design calls for, no harm is done. But the dimensions used to plan the sprinkler system must be accurate to within a foot or so. You will be working with sprinkler heads that are designed to close tolerances. If you discover an error of 5 feet when you are installing the heads, you may have to go back to the drawing board and redesign that part of the system.

The lower branches of trees can interfere with a spray pattern. Note the height of these branches and any other aerial obstacles on the plan. Also note the locations of curbs. Sprinkler heads placed too close to an uncurbed street or driveway will be constantly broken off; place heads at least 3 feet from the street.

Locate valve manifolds where they are convenient to reach, and where they will not be within a spray pattern. Mark off irrigation areas that have different needs for water. Each of these areas must be controlled separately, to meet its own water requirements.

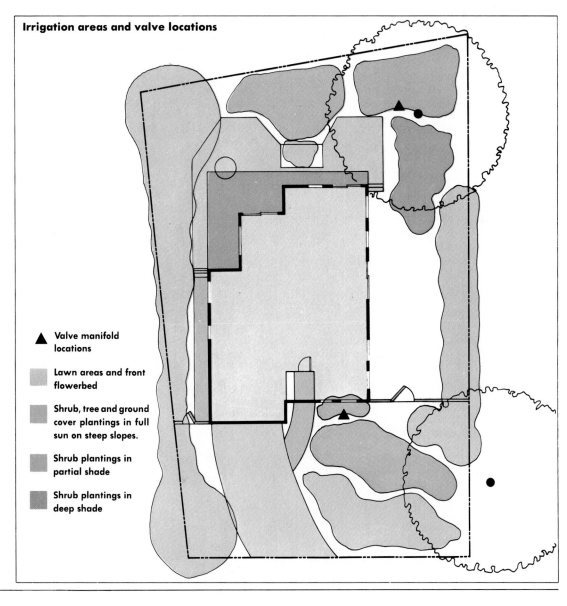

Irrigation areas and valve locations

▲ Valve manifold locations

Lawn areas and front flowerbed

Shrub, tree and ground cover plantings in full sun on steep slopes.

Shrub plantings in partial shade

Shrub plantings in deep shade

Position the manifolds

The sprinkler system manifold is composed of a group of valves that control the sprinkler system. The valves should be located in a convenient spot near an entrance to the house, where you can turn them on and off without getting yourself wet.

If you are using a controller to open and close valves for you, you can position the valves anywhere. (See box).

Selecting sprinkler heads

Decide which sections of your yard you will want to water separately from other sections; these areas will be on separate circuits. Lawns need water more frequently than shrubs; annual beds and rose beds have different water needs.

Now decide which areas you want to keep dry: You will want to keep water off the side of your house, and off fences; fences and walls are bleached or discolored by water from sprinklers. Use the information in the catalogs to choose heads that will fit your plan. Use a compass to plot the pattern covered by each head. The catalog will tell you the shape and size of each head's pattern.

Select heads that use less than 60 percent of the water pressure you measured. This way there will be adequate pressure for the sprinklers even when you are taking a shower or washing dishes.

Sprinkler head spray patterns

Lawn heads sit flush with lawn so that mowers clear them. They are available in stationary or pop-up models.

Shrub heads are on risers to clear shrubbery. As the shrubbery grows, install longer risers to keep the heads clear of foliage.

Spacing

Space heads so that each one is just touched by the water thrown by adjacent heads. This 100 percent overlap is required to get the same amount of water on each spot of the yard. When you're fitting odd corners, add an extra head, if need be, rather than stretch the pattern—stretching the distance between heads is the mistake most commonly made in sprinkler system design. One small portion of the lawn may get only half as much water as the rest of the lawn—and you will have to water the entire lawn twice as long to keep that small portion green.

As you decide on each head, write the catalog number of that head next to its location on the plan.

Controllers

A sprinkler system can be controlled manually or automatically. A fully automated system has a controller to turn the valves on and off.

The controller will turn on each circuit at the time you select and on the days you select, and it will leave the circuit on for the length of time you select. If you wish, you can have the controller do all your watering in the early morning hours, as most parks and golf courses do.

There are two advantages to watering at night: one is that nobody else is using water at this time, so you get the maximum pressure; in some neighborhoods, this is important.

The other advantage is that you don't have to worry about keeping paths or patios dry. You can use fewer, larger heads that throw water all across the yard. At five o'clock in the morning, nobody cares. Although larger heads are more expensive, there is an overall savings in money because you use far fewer of them.

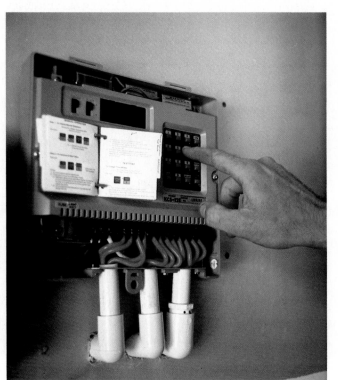

This automatic sprinkler controller is a product of solid-state technology. It is programmed by pushing buttons, like a small computer. Controllers can be set to turn on any circuit when you wish, at any time of day, and turn it off after a set period of time. Other types of controllers work like electric clocks, with wheels that are set for the day, hour, and duration of the irrigation cycle.

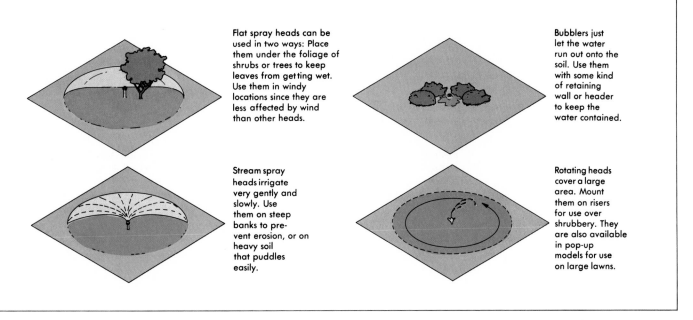

Flat spray heads can be used in two ways: Place them under the foliage of shrubs or trees to keep leaves from getting wet. Use them in windy locations since they are less affected by wind than other heads.

Bubblers just let the water run out onto the soil. Use them with some kind of retaining wall or header to keep the water contained.

Stream spray heads irrigate very gently and slowly. Use them on steep banks to prevent erosion, or on heavy soil that puddles easily.

Rotating heads cover a large area. Mount them on risers for use over shrubbery. They are also available in pop-up models for use on large lawns.

Position the sprinkler heads so that every spot being irrigated is covered by at least two heads. If the catalog description of the head tells you how far apart to space the heads, follow those instructions. Otherwise, space the heads so that the water thrown from each head touches the heads adjacent to it. Draw the spray pattern for each head with a compass.

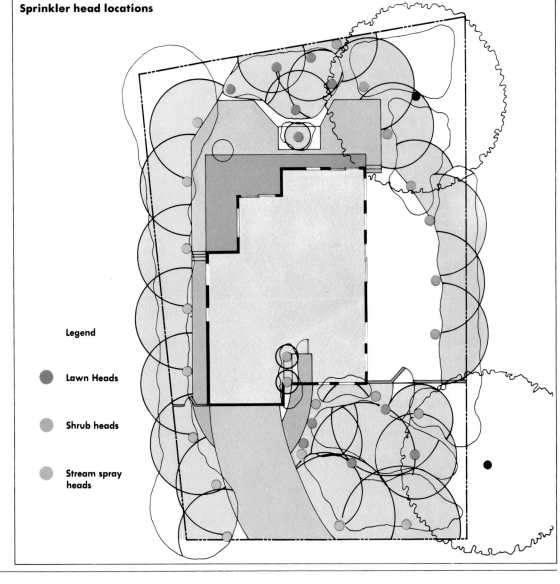

Sprinkler head locations

Legend

● Lawn Heads

● Shrub heads

● Stream spray heads

Valves

Some of the different types of valves used in sprinkler systems are:

Gate valves are inexpensive and simple in operation; a "gate" within the valve slides up and down to open or close the valve. They are used as shut-off valves and in locations that get only occasional use.

Anti-siphon valves, also called vacuum breakers, allow air to enter the highest point of an irrigation system to break any possible vacuum that could siphon water from the garden back into the main water supply.

Manual control valves are usually globe valves, the same type of valve that is used in faucets in the house. Globe valves shut off the flow of water by pressing a soft disc against a smooth valve seat. A manual control valve controls a sprinkler circuit. All the valves for a front or back yard are usually located in one location, in a *valve manifold*, for convenience. Sometimes anti-siphon valves and manual control valves are combined in one valve body.

Remote control valves are used with an automatic controller. They are usually electrically controlled by a solenoid mounted on the valve. Remote control valves are buried in a valve box in any convenient spot, rather than being grouped together in a manifold.

The finished plan shows all the heads and valves connected by pipes. Each circuit is controlled by a valve. In operation, only one circuit is turned on at a time. We left the catalog numbers and the fitting and pipe sizes off this plan for clarity, but your finished plan should show all the parts you will need, including numbers and sizes.

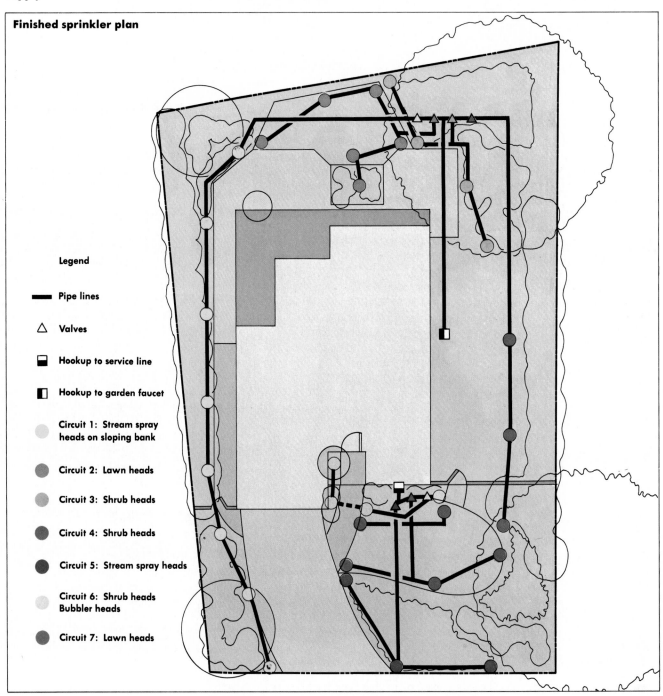

Finished sprinkler plan

Legend

— Pipe lines

△ Valves

▣ Hookup to service line

▮ Hookup to garden faucet

○ Circuit 1: Stream spray heads on sloping bank

● Circuit 2: Lawn heads

○ Circuit 3: Shrub heads

● Circuit 4: Shrub heads

● Circuit 5: Stream spray heads

○ Circuit 6: Shrub heads Bubbler heads

● Circuit 7: Lawn heads

PVC pipe ratings

Polyvinyl chloride (PVC) pipe is manufactured under two different rating systems: schedule rating and class rating. *Schedule-rated* pipe, which is rated like iron pipe, has walls that are uniform in thickness no matter what the pipes' diameters are. This kind of pipe usually is connected by threaded fittings.

With *SDR-PR* PVC pipe (commonly called *class-rated*), the walls are thicker when the diameter is greater; this means that its pressure rating remains the same no matter what the diameter. The class rating idicates the strength. Class 200 PVC pipe, for example, has a bursting strength of 200 pounds of pressure per square inch.

Schedule-rated pipe is stronger in the smaller diameters (under 1½ inches). Class-rated pipe is stronger in the larger diameters.

Pipe classes that are common in home sprinkler systems are class 315, class 200, class 160, and schedule 40. Class 200 is commonly used for lateral lines; class 160 is a less expensive alternative. Schedule 40 pipe often is chosen for main lines and lines that bear pressure.

Occasionally, schedule 80 PVC is specified where extra strength is needed—for example, risers, which can get kicked and broken, benefit from the additional strength.

Designing the circuits

A circuit is a series of sprinkler heads controlled by a single valve and connected by pipes. Three rules govern the way you will design the circuits in your system:

1. All areas covered by one circuit must be watered together. Do not include a rose bed and a lawn on the same circuit.

2. All the heads on a single circuit must use less than 75 percent of the available flow rate. The flow rate of each head is included in its catalog description. Add up the flow rates of all the heads; the total must be less than 75 percent of the flow rate for your home. In operation, only one circuit is turned on at a time.

3. Only one type of head can be on a single circuit. That is, you cannot put a bubbler on a circuit with a rotating head; you cannot put a rotating head on a circuit with a lawn head.

Connect the sprinkler heads with pipe lines, and connect these lines to the manifold. Try to avoid running lines under walks or close to trees.

Selecting valves and pipe

Check your local plumbing codes for any special restrictions on types or positioning of valves. Choose anti-syphoning valves for most locations. These prevent an accidental suctioning of water (containing fertilizer or pesticides) from the lawn back into the house supply.

Use *Chart 3* to find the size valve you need for each circuit, depending on the combined flow rates of all the heads on that circuit. Write the catalog number of the valve on the plan. Use the same chart to select pipe sizes. The main feeder line from the house service line to the manifold should be the same size as the largest valve in the manifold. If the length of the feeder line is greater than 100 feet, specify a pipe one size larger than the largest valve—even if this makes the feeder line larger than the service line to which it connects.

Next to each pipe length on the plan, write its size.

List fittings

Using the manifold and head detail drawing, write the size and name of each fitting on the plan.

Locate the controller

If you are going to use a controller, choose a weatherproof location for it, such as the garage. Plan a route for the wire that will connect the controller to the valves.

Make a parts list

On a separate piece of paper, list the valves, heads, fittings and pipe you need. As you "take off" each piece, circle its name on the plan so that you won't count it again.

List the controller, a can of PVC cement, and a hacksaw. Now you can see how much the system is going to cost—and now you are ready to buy your parts.

Parts List for Sprinkler System

Item	Quantity	Catalog Number	Description	Price per Each	Total Price	Delivered
Valves	1		1" gate valve			
	1		1¼" gate valve			
	6	ASV 200 A	¾" manual anti-siphon angle valve			
	1	ASV 200 B	1" manual anti-siphon angle valve			
Heads	5	P1500Q	¼ circle pop-up brass lawn head			
	5	P1500H	½ circle pop-up brass lawn head			
	1	P1500F	Full circle pop-up brass lawn head			
	1	SS2800Q	¼ circle stream spray shrub head			
	2	S1200 ES	End strip shrub spray head			
	2	B1250	Shrub bubbler head			
Riser Assemblies	12		½" × 6" cut-off risers (lawn heads)			
	22		½" × 8" schedule 80 PVC risers			
	34		½" × 4" flex risers			
	34		½" schedule 80 PVC threaded couplings			
Pipe	60'		1¼" schedule 40 PVC pipe			
	50'		1" class 200 PVC pipe			
	380'		¾" class 200 PVC pipe			
	220'		½" class 200 PVC pipe			

This is a partial list of parts for the system at left. Use this as a guide to make a list for your own system.

Chart 3: Valve and pipe size

Maximum GPM	Valve or pipe size
14	¾"
25	1"
40	1¼"

Courtesy of Rain Bird Sprinkler Mfg. Corp.

Sprinkler Installation

Buy the parts you need and gather your tools together. Now you are ready to install the sprinkler system. The line from the house service line to the valves holds pressure; it is a "live" line. Up to the valves, heavier pipe and fittings are used, and building codes are more strict. You may wish to hire a plumber to install this portion of your system.

To install the manifold, first turn off the water to the house. Cut a 1¼-inch section from the service pipe and install a slip compression tee (you don't have to thread the cut pipe ends). Install a length of pipe and a valve in a valve box. Now you can

turn the house water back on. Run lines to the manifold locations and install the manifolds. The illustrations may look complicated, but if you start from the upstream end and just add one piece at a time, you will find the process easier than you might have imagined.

Now close the valves, open the shut-off valve, and test the manifold for leaks.

Install the controller

If you are using a controller, install it according to the manufacturer's instructions, and lay the connecting wire to the valves. Most controllers run on a voltage that's low enough (24 volts) to let you bury the wire directly, without conduit.

Lay out the system

Drive a stake into the ground at each head location. Then use agricultural lime to draw lines on the ground where the pipes will go.

Trenching

You can trench by hand, or you can rent a trencher.

If you are laying pipe through an existing lawn, cut the sod and lay it aside; then when you are through, replace it.

Make the ditches at least 12 inches deep. If you will be tilling over them, make them at least 16 inches deep. If you are in an area where the ground freezes, you need

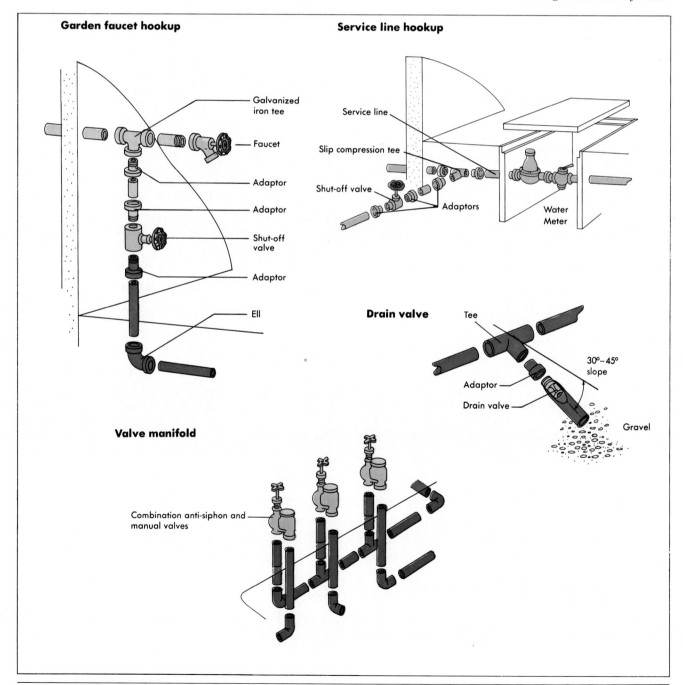

Garden faucet hookup

Galvanized iron tee
Faucet
Adaptor
Adaptor
Shut-off valve
Adaptor
Ell

Service line hookup

Service line
Slip compression tee
Shut-off valve
Adaptors
Water Meter

Drain valve

Tee
30°–45° slope
Adaptor
Drain valve
Gravel

Valve manifold

Combination anti-siphon and manual valves

not lay the pipe beneath the frost line; however, you should install automatic drain valves (see drain valve detail).

Assembling the System

Tie the risers to the stakes you drove at the sprinkler head locations. Work backward to the manifold, assembling the pipe and fittings (leave the heads off). When it is all assembled and the last joint has had time to set, turn on the water to flush out any pieces of dirt or stones from the pipes. Then attach the heads.

Test the system

Turn on each circuit one by one; inspect the pattern carefully, to make sure that every part of the ground is getting adequate coverage. At this point it's easy to add additional heads where they are needed.

Backfill

Once you are sure that your sprinkler system will operate in conformance with your design, fill the trenches with the soil you removed. Stop just short of the top, remove the heads again, and slowly run water through all the circuits—the water will fill the ditches and help settle the backfill soil more completely, which will prevent settling and low spots later on. Put the heads back on, finish filling the trench, clean up your mess, and you have a brand-new sprinkler system.

Head on riser

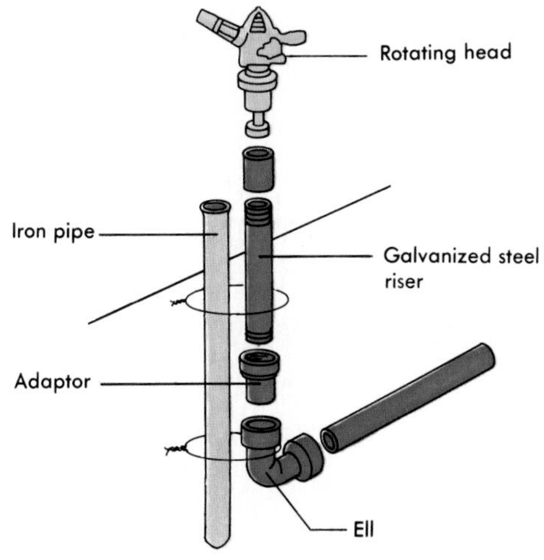

- Rotating head
- Iron pipe
- Galvanized steel riser
- Adaptor
- Ell

Lawn head

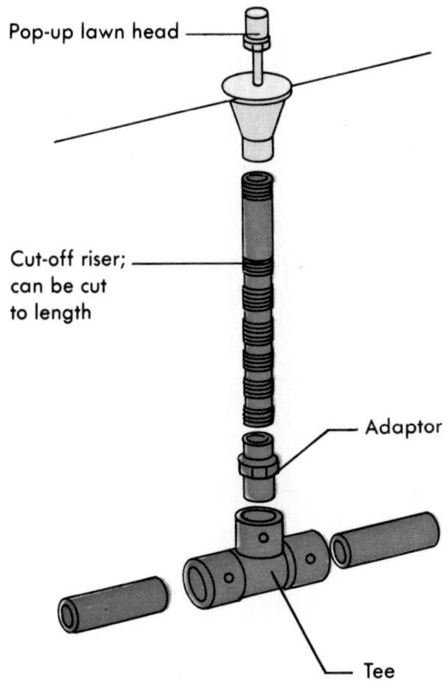

- Pop-up lawn head
- Cut-off riser; can be cut to length
- Adaptor
- Tee

Making PVC Connections

Class 200 PVC (polyvinyl chloride) pipe is the type most commonly used for sprinkler systems. It is lightweight, semi-rigid, and easy to work with.

Cut the pipe to length with a hacksaw and scrape the edges to remove any burrs. Wipe cement (there is a dauber in the cap) on the outside of the pipe and the inside of the fitting. Slide the fitting onto the pipe as far as it will go and turn it ¼ turn to smear cement around the conneciton. Wipe off any excess cement immediately. This is important because the cement is actually a solvent. A large amount left on the outside of the pipe will eat into it and weaken it.

Going under walks

If you have to put pipe under walks or driveways, the easiest method is to: dig the ditch on both sides of the walk; cap both ends of a length of 1-inch galvanized pipe; and drive the pipe under the walk with a sledge hammer. Attach the PVC piping to this piece.

STEP 7: IMPROVING SOIL

How much you need to improve your soil depends on what condition it was in when you began your landscaping project. If it was growing a healthy garden—or even a healthy weed crop—and if there are no problems with water puddling up, you may not need to do much at all.

Organic matter

Organic matter, one of the best things you can do for your garden, will improve almost any soil. It holds on to water and nutrients like a sponge, increasing the soil's capacity for them; it separates soil particles, opening and loosening the soil; and, as it breaks down into humus, it forms glue-like materials that stick soil particles together into little crumbs, making the soil soft and friable.

Most organic materials are beneficial to your soil. Wood by-products like sawdust and composted bark are widely available; so are ground corn cobs and peatmoss. You may be able to find many other materials—including the farmer's standby, manure—in your area that are available for the hauling or at a low price.

Spread the organic matter on the surface of the soil between 1 and 4 inches deep. It is better to add a few inches each year than to try to add too much at once. However, the effects of a single addition of organic matter will last for years.

If the organic matter does not already have added nitrogen, add an additional 2 pounds of ammonium sulfate (or its equivalent) per 100 square feet. This will prevent the organic matter from tying up the available nitrogen in the soil as it decomposes.

Gypsum

If you have a very sticky clay soil that drains slowly, gypsum might help to improve its structure. Try mixing some into the soil in a small area at a rate of about 5 pounds per 100 square feet. If it works, it will improve the drainage almost immediately. Check by performing the drainage test on page 75.

Lime

If you live east of the 100th meridian, there is a good chance that your soil will be benefited by lime. If you already had a soil analysis done, you probably were told how much lime to add. If you haven't had a soil analysis, ask at your local nursery whether your soil needs lime. Use the chart below as a rough guide for how much lime to add.

Fertilizers

Almost all soils are benefited by the addition of fertilizer. Apply 20 pounds per 1000 square feet of a general-purpose 8-8-8 fertilizer, or its equivalent.

Tilling

After you have spread these materials evenly over the surface of the ground, the next step is to till them into the soil. Tilling is most easily accomplished with a rented rototiller. Rent the largest one you can; the heavier the machine, the easier the work. Light rototillers are for soft soil, like that vegetable garden tilled only last year.

You only need to till the areas where you will plant lawn or bedding plants.

Most rototillers stir the soil to a depth of about 6 inches. It *is* important to get down this deep. If your soil is hard, there are a number of ways to till it deeply.

First, make sure the soil is sufficiently moist before you begin. If it hasn't rained recently, water the soil thoroughly, then wait a few days to let the soil drain before you start tilling. When a clod crumbles in your fist instead of deforming, the soil is ready to work.

Second, go over the soil with the rototiller a number of times. Each time, you will till a little deeper.

Third, if all else fails, hire a contractor or a farmer to till for you with a tractor-mounted tiller.

Pounds of limestone needed to bring the soil to a pH of 6.5			
	Pounds of limestone per hundred square feet		
pH	Sandy Loam	Loam	Clay Loam
4.0	11.5	16	23
4.5	9.5	13.5	19.5
5.0	8	10.5	15
5.5	6	8	10.5
6.0	3	4	5.5

You can obtain a more rapid reaction by the use of hydrated lime. Use three-fourths as much as is recommended for limestone.

STEP 8: FINISH LEVEL

Once you have installed the headers and dug most of the trenches, it's time to finish off the surface of the soil. In all but the lawn areas, just a final raking will do. Use the headers as elevation guides. If the soil hasn't yet been settled by rainfall or irrigation, leave it about an inch higher than the headers to compensate for later settling.

For the lawn, a finer touch is needed. Use a wooden or aluminum leveling rake with an extra-wide head and long handle to comb any rocks or clods larger than about ½ inch from the surface 2 inches. Level the ground even with headers, walks,

**Above: This rented landscaper's rake simplifies leveling.
Below: Settle the soil with a roller, then rake it again. Repeat until the ground stays level after rolling.**

STEP 9: PLANT LARGER PLANTS

and patios if you are going to seed your lawn, or level it ¾ inch below the surface if you are going to lay sod. Crown it slightly in the center to allow for good drainage and possible future settling, especially if the soil has not yet been settled by rainfall.

Now wet down the lawn area, roll it with a lawn roller, and level it again. Repeat this process until there are no low spots for the roller to press down against.

If your timing has been right, the nursery delivered your plants just as you finished leveling the area you plan to put them in. Now gather them all on the patio and spread out your landscape plan.

Spotting

Using the plan as a guide, place the plants exactly where you want them to grow. (If you will be putting in some bare-root trees or shrubs, for the moment substitute stakes.) This is the last time you will have

a chance to change your mind without having to work hard for the privilege.

Spot all the plants in an area at once. Now walk around and eye the planting critically. Remember that the plants will grow. Will that laurel crowd the boxwood hedge in a couple of years? Better move it out another 2 feet.

At first, your planting will look thin, but have patience; a landscape, like any living thing, must begin as an infant and grow slowly into the full glory of its ma-

As you spot plants, imagine them as they will look in five years. When you are sure you have everything just where you want it, set the plants in the ground exactly where you spotted them. At this point, moving plants is as easy as moving furniture; it will be difficult to move them later.

turity. Place your plants just close together enough so that the garden will look full in five years.

Planting

The soil has probably not been rototilled where the larger plants are to be installed. Irrigate if it is dry, then wait a day or so for the soil to drain before you plant. This will make digging infinitely easier.

In general, planting holes should be as deep as the rootball, and twice as wide. Set the plant aside and dig the hole exactly where you spotted it. If your soil is a heavy clay, add a little soil amendment to the soil you remove from the hole. Sprinkle some fertilizer (2 tablespoons of 8-8-8 for a 1-gallon plant; ¼ cup for a 5-gallon plant; and ½ cup for a 15-gallon plant) into the hole and scratch it into the soil.

Remove the plant from the container. Plastic cans and crimped metal cans are designed so that you can knock out the plant without cutting the can, although straight-sided metal cans will usually have to be cut. Nurseries sell a tool for cutting cans. If you have enough cans to cut, it may be worth the investment.

Since 15-gallon cans are heavy and awkward to handle, a good way to cut them is by removing the bottom with a hatchet, and then using the handles on the can to put the tree in the hole. When the tree is just where you want it, cut off the rest of the can without disturbing the tree.

Once the plant is out of the can, either tease the roots around the outside of the rootball, or slash them across the bottom and, with 3 vertical cuts, up the sides. This quick pruning stimulates new root growth into the soil. In the case of trees, this is especially important, otherwise the roots circling the outside of the rootball may still be in the same place 15 years from now, choking the trunk.

Place the plant in the hole so that the top of the rootball is level with, or even slightly above, ground level. This drains water away from the base of the plant, and helps to prevent crown rot.

If you are planting ball-and-burlap plants, place the plant in the hole, keeping the twine and burlap in place. Cut the twine, then open the top of the burlap and fold it back. This way, the burlap and twine will be buried when you backfill the hole.

If you are planting bareroot plants, trim off any broken or extra-long roots. Place the plant in the hole, keeping the top root just below ground level. As you fill the hole, work the soil between the roots with your fingers to fill any voids.

Puddling in

No matter what type of plant you're planting, you need to build a basin around the hole you just backfilled. Make a generous basin—it should be deep enough to allow one filling with a hose to saturate the entire root area and the soil around it; and it should be strong enough to let you water in it for a few weeks without it falling apart.

Now fill each basin with water. As it soaks in and the backfill soil becomes soupy mud, you can correct the plant's position, if desired. Shake it gently to release any trapped air, and lift it or turn it so that it is positioned exactly as you wish.

Staking

Drive stakes in against the outside of the rootball, deep into undisturbed soil at the bottom of the hole. (If you're planting trees, don't use the stake that came in the can—that's a training stake, and much too light for your purposes now.)

Tie the tree to the stake as low as you can and still have the stake support the tree. Use only one tie. Your aim is for the tree to outgrow the need for the stake, eventually. So, stake it in such a way that it can move in the wind; movement strengthens both the trunk and the root system.

Remove the bottom of large trees before placing them in the planting hole. You can use the handles on the can to move the tree, and the can protects the rootball if you have to lift it in and out of the hole several times.

Don't remove the burlap wrapping of a ball-and-burlap plant. Fold it back and bury the wrapping and twine as you backfill the hole. Be careful not to break the rootball as you handle the unwrapped plant.

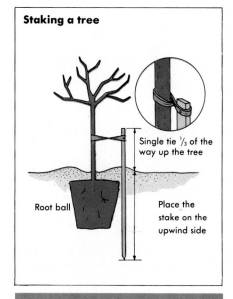

Staking a tree

Single tie ⅓ of the way up the tree

Root ball

Place the stake on the upwind side

STEP 10:
PLANT LAWNS AND GROUND COVERS

Once planted, these areas are fragile. We have saved them for last so that you won't be tempted to shortcut across the new lawn and damage it.

Grounds covers and bedding plants

Usually, these are planted from flats into tilled soil. Plant in rows, working backwards so that you don't have to worry about stepping on what you have just planted. If the soil is soft, you can just use your hands to plant. Plant a little low, so that water will puddle at the base of each plant when you water them. Water from a watering can or a slow hose at the base of each plant. Not only does the water wet the plants, but it also settles them into the soil.

Seeding a lawn

Level and roll the lawn area one more time to remove any footprints. Water it thoroughly if it has dried out.

Spread the seed carefully with a rented spreader (most nurseries will lend them to people who buy seed). Most seeds are sown at a rate of about 1 to 2 pounds per 1000 square feet; check with your dealer for the proper rate for your seed.

Scratch the seed into the soil by dragging a rake across the lawn. A spring-toothed lawn rake does this job well. Do not pile the seed up in little piles with a back-and-forth motion; just drag the rake evenly from one end to the other.

Roll with a light lawn roller (half filled with water) to press the seed into the soil.

Spread a mulch about ⅛ inch deep over the lawn. Sawdust works well. The purpose of the mulch is to keep the seed damp; don't make it so deep that it buries the seed forever. Special spreaders are available from many nurseries to spread the mulch.

Do whatever is necessary to keep traffic off the lawn for a few weeks.

It is very important to keep the mulch damp for the next couple of weeks. If it dries out, newly germinated seedlings can die very quickly. Water gently by hand to avoid washing out the seeds. However, once most of the seed has germinated, let the surface of the soil dry out between waterings—at this stage, the new seedlings are very susceptible to fungus diseases, and they will succumb more quickly in wet conditions.

Mow your new lawn as soon as it needs mowing. If you plan to keep it at 2 inches, mow as soon as it reaches 3 inches. Use a sharp, reel-type mower for the first few cuttings to avoid pulling out the young plants.

Sodding a lawn

Level and roll the ground one more time, and water it if it has dried out. Sod is cut with ¾ inch of soil attached, so prepare the

Lawns: Seed vs. Sod

You have your choice of planting seed or buying a sod lawn. Either choice can give a beautiful lawn if you are careful and attentive to details.

Seed:
Is cheaper—much cheaper if you provide the labor.
Gives you more choice of grass variety and mix.
Is quicker and easier work.

Sod:
Is instant lawn.
Can be installed any time of year.
Stops erosion and soil splash problems instantly.
Is more sure; there is less chance of failure.

Whether you choose to seed or sod, in a year your lawn will look as nice as this one. Prepare the soil carefully and choose grass that is suited to your part of the country. This will lay the foundation for a beautiful and trouble-free lawn.

Sodding produces an instant lawn. Start at an edge and lay the sod in straight rows, staggering the joints like a brick wall. The concrete edging shown here does double duty as a header and a mowing strip, making both mowing and edging the lawn easier. Daily watering is important in dry weather until the sod is established.

ground level ¾ inch lower than you want the finished lawn. It's just as important to prepare the soil carefully with a sodded lawn as with a seeded one.

Have the sod delivered as close to where it will be laid as possible, even if this means removing a section of fence. In summer, the sod should not stand on the pallet any more than one day, so plan to lay it the day it is delivered.

Most commonly, sod is delivered in rolls that measure 18 inches wide by 6 feet long, stacked on a pallet. The delivery truck tows a fork lift that will set the pallet anywhere you want (provided that it can reach).

Start laying the sod at the edge of a header or patio. Work forward so that you are standing on the newly laid sod; if you work backward, your footprints will disturb the ground. Unroll a strip, then dig your fingers into the grass and tug it to-

wards you to snug it up against the header or the edge of the adjacent strip of sod. Do not stretch it; it will shrink slightly as it lies, and cracks between strips will dry out and die.

Stagger the joints as you would stagger the bricks in a brick wall. If you are laying the sod on a slope, put the strips *across* the slope so that the cracks between strips won't erode.

If the weather is hot and dry and you want to make quite sure that the cracks between strips don't dry out, dribble fine sand into the cracks. However, this measure is usually not necessary if you snug the strips tightly.

Mow your newly sodded lawn when it needs it, but otherwise keep traffic off. Water daily (unless it rains) until the sod is established—usually about 3 weeks in warm weather. To determine whether it is established, tug gently at a corner. If

the roots have grown into the native soil and the new sod is knit into the ground, it is established. (For extensive details on lawns and ground covers, see Ortho's books, *All About Lawns* and *All About Ground Covers*.)

STEP 11: CLEAN-UP

This step won't be too great a job if you have been cleaning up after each step. Often, extra materials (although not sod) can be returned for credit, or give them to neighbors.

Be thorough in your clean-up. Those little piles of rock or lumber will have a tendency to take up permanent residence if you don't get rid of them now. A thorough clean-up gives your landscaping job a professional finish. For that final touch, hose down all wood and concrete surfaces with a jet nozzle.

STEP 12: AFTERCARE

Your new plants don't really belong to the site until they have their roots well established in the native soil. Until then, they are still container plants or ball-and-burlap plants, and will dry up quickly on a hot day. Check the rootball daily—it can dry out even though the soil immediately adjacent to it is damp.

Water the larger plants by filling their basins with water, as needed, even if you have a new sprinkler system that you are dying to use. Once the plants are established (about 6 weeks), scatter the basins and place the plants on a regular irrigation schedule.

Congratulations! You are now the parent of a baby garden that will grow, ripen, and mature to give you increased pleasure as the years pass.

The reward for all your hard work is a beautiful garden. It will give you all the more pleasure over the years because you designed and installed it yourself. The design of this carefully thought-out garden reflects its owner's taste as well as providing a serene and secluded retreat.

Index

Italics indicate photographs or illustrations